The EWT Coach

WRITING

by Sheila C. Crowell
& Ellen D. Kolba

EDUCATIONAL DESIGN, INC.   EDI 211

ACKNOWLEDGMENTS

We gratefully acknowledge permission to use the state topics on the "homeless" (in lesson 4) and "parents can choose friends" (in lesson 7). Our students prepared for the remake of the EWT by writing essays on these topics. In addition, we acknowledge the state of New Jersey's permission to reproduce the Scoring Guide (in Lesson 2), which has been adapted for reasons of space. Showing students how to use the State guidelines empowers them as thinkers and writers.

TABLE OF CONTENTS

Part 1 of the Writing Test

1. THE ESSAY TEST

What is the New Jersey EWT (Early Warning Test) in Writing like?

It's a test in two parts. The first part of the test asks you to write an essay. This part of the test is covered in the first part of this book.

The second part of the test is made up of sample essays that contain errors in usage, mechanics, and sentence construction. Each essay is followed by multiple-choice questions that ask you to identify and correct the essay's errors. This part of the test is covered in the second part of this book.

What kind of essay do I have to write for the first part of the test?

You will be asked to write an essay that does one of the following:

- Offers a solution to a problem

- Tells about causes and/or effects

- Expresses a point of view on a controversial issue

Even though you will one write only one of these compositions for the test, you need to practice writing all three.

Is there any special information I need to know in order to write an EWT essay?

No. You don't need to know any special facts.

It helps to be a good observer and to be aware of what is going on around you. For example, are there any problems that students are concerned about in your school? Can you think of a solution to one of these problems? What are some of the important issues that concern you, your family, or your community? What is your opinion about these issues? Have you ever wondered about what makes things happen or what happens as the result of something?

The exercises in this book will help you learn more about dealing with the kinds of topics you may be tested on.

How much time do I have?

You will have 40 minutes to complete your essay. If you use the first 5 minutes of the test to plan your essay and the last 5 minutes to proofread the essay, you will have 30 minutes in which to write.

Is there a place on the test for prewriting and planning?

You can make notes, lists, outlines, and writing maps on the back of the instructions sheet.

WARNING: Don't leave good ideas on the planning sheet! Your prewriting notes will not be included in the scoring of your essay. Read over your notes before you begin writing, and circle or underline all the ideas you are going to use. When you proofread your essay, be sure that you have included everything you meant to put in. You can make a check mark beside each idea that you included.

Does neatness count?

Of course, if no one can read your essay, it can't be scored at all. But the test scorers mainly want to know how well you write, not how neatly you write.

How will my essay be scored?

The State of New Jersey uses a special scoring method called the Registered Holistic Scoring Method (RHSM) to evaluate essays. You will learn how it works in the next chapter in this book.

2. HOW YOUR ESSAY WILL BE SCORED

A good way to begin preparing for the writing test is to look at sample student essays and see how you would score them. This will help you understand what scorers expect.

In this chapter, you will look at 6 essays and score them, just as if you were a real scorer for the test.

What does a scorer look for?

A scorer looks for all the following things:

- **CONTENT/ORGANIZATION.** What does the writer have to say about the topic? How well are these ideas organized?

- **USAGE.** Does the writer follow the rules of standard English usage?

- **SENTENCE CONSTRUCTION.** Are the sentences correct, interesting, and varied? Do they make sense?

- **MECHANICS.** How correct is the writer's spelling, capitalization, and punctuation?

Content and organization are considered the most important. That is why they come first in the list.

How is an essay scored?

The scoring scale is from 1 (lowest) to 6 (highest). Each essay is read by two scorers; then the scores are added. Combined scores can range from 2 to 12. When two readers each give an essay a 6, the top score is 12.

To pass the EWT, the essay needs to show an "Adequate Command" of written language, which is usually an 8 (or two 4s).

The lowest possible score is no score. An essay receives the score NSR (Non-Scorable Response) for one of the following reasons:

- The student wrote so little that the scorer could not judge the writing.

- The essay was not on the assigned topic.

- The essay was written in a language other than English.

- The answer folder was blank, or the student refused to write.

STUDYING MODEL ESSAYS

On the next two pages you will see a Scoring Guide chart like the one scorers actually use. You will use the guidelines on the chart to score the six model essays that follow.

Read the guidelines first. Then read the essays. When you have finished, give each essay a score. Then, working with a partner, tell why you gave each essay the score you did. Listen to the reasons your partner gave. Make any changes in scores that you wish, and discuss the results with the rest of the class.

SCORING GUIDE

Score: 1

This essay shows an **INADEQUATE COMMAND** of written language.
A very poor essay.

CONTENT / ORGANIZATION

- May not have an opening or a closing
- Hardly any real response to the topic—focus is unclear
- No planning—essay is disorganized and hard to understand
- Details—if any—do not seem to belong with the topic

USAGE

- Many usage errors: problems in subject-verb agreement, pronoun usage, word choice, modifiers, etc.

SENTENCE CONSTRUCTION

- Many incomplete, incorrect, or hard-to-understand sentences

MECHANICS

- Many errors in spelling, capitalization, and punctuation make the essay difficult to read and understand

Score: 2

This essay shows a **LIMITED COMMAND** of written language.
A poor essay.

CONTENT / ORGANIZATION

- May not have an opening or a closing
- Some attempt to focus, but may drift away from the topic
- Some planning—the writer has tried to organize her or his ideas. But there are few transitions or poor transitions from thought to thought
- Details are not elaborated or developed (the writer doesn't explain each detail fully)

USAGE

- Many errors

SENTENCE CONSTRUCTION

- Sentences are dull and not varied
- Many errors in sentence construction

MECHANICS

- Many serious errors in spelling, capitalization, and punctuation

Score: 3

This essay shows a **PARTIAL COMMAND** of written language.
An unsatisfactory essay.

CONTENT / ORGANIZATION

- May or may not have an opening or a closing
- Usually has a single focus
- May be somewhat organized, but lacks consistent organization. Some transitions between ideas may be missing
- Details not developed or poorly developed: may say the same thing in two or three different ways

USAGE

- May have a pattern of errors in one area

SENTENCE CONSTRUCTION

- Very few sentences are varied
- May contain some errors in construction

MECHANICS

- May contain a pattern of errors in spelling, capitalization, or punctuation

10

Score: 4

This essay shows an *ADEQUATE COMMAND* of written language. A satisfactory essay.

CONTENT / ORGANIZATION

- Usually has an opening and a closing
- Sticks to the topic
- Is organized and has transitions, but ideas may be only loosely connected and the writer may ramble
- Development of ideas is often uneven—some are elaborated and some are not

USAGE

- Some errors, but no consistent pattern
- Errors don't interfere with meaning

SENTENCE CONSTRUCTION

- Generally correct
- Sentences show some variety

MECHANICS

- May have some spelling, capitalization, and punctuation errors. However, the errors don't form a pattern and don't interfere with meaning

Score: 5

This essay shows a *STRONG COMMAND* of written language. A very good essay.

CONTENT/ ORGANIZATION

- Has an opening and a closing
- Stays focused and on topic, and has a sense of completeness and unity. Has development of key ideas
- Ideas progress logically. Writer may take some risks by adding strong description or narration
- Details are effective and varied

USAGE

- Few errors in usage

SENTENCE CONSTRUCTION

- Few errors
- Sentences are varied and interesting

MECHANICS

- Very few errors in spelling, capitalization, or punctuation

Score: 6

This essay shows a *SUPERIOR COMMAND* of written language. A *WOW!* essay

CONTENT/ ORGANIZATION

- Has an opening and a closing
- Stays strongly focused and on topic, and has a sense of completeness and unity. Key ideas are very well developed
- Ideas progress logically. Groups of ideas are strongly connected. Writer may take successful risks by adding strong description or narration
- Details are effective, well described, vivid, and make their point well

USAGE

- Few errors or none

SENTENCE CONSTRUCTION

- Few errors or none
- Sentences are varied and effective, advanced and sophisticated in style

MECHANICS

- Few errors or none in spelling, capitalization, or punctuation

11

DIRECTIONS: Read the following description of a writing task. Then read the two essays that were written on this topic.

When you have finished, give each essay a score and give your reasons. Then, working with a partner, tell why you gave each essay the score you did. Listen to the reasons your partner gave. Make any changes in scores and reasons that you wish.

> Do you think parents should have the right to make rules about who their children's friends can be? Think about this issue and decide how you feel about it. Then write a letter to a teen magazine giving your opinion.

ESSAY 1

Dear Editor:

(1)   I feel parents shouldn't choose your friends. When your in eighth grade. Because eighth graders are at an age when they mature. We have a right to choose who we want to be freinds with.

(2)   Here are the reasons I think this way. First, eighth graders are at an age when they start to grow up and mature alot. Some eighth-grade boys are ready to start shaving. We should know who to choose to hang around with. We have a right to make our own decisions.

(3)   Second, eighth graders got a right to choose who they want to be friends with. Parents shouldn't try to pick kids friends because they might pick the wrong friend.

(4)   In conclusion, I really feel parents shouldn't choose your friends.

Score: _____

Reasons: _____

_____

_____

_____

ESSAY 2

Dear Editor:

(1)   I am writing to you about the question of whether parents should say who their children can spend time with. As an eighth-grader, I think that teenagers should be allowed to choose their own friends. Even though we are still not adults and we don't always know who our real friends are, our parents should not tell us that we can't hang out with someone without explaining why.

(2)   Parents should trust us. They should know that we know what's wrong and what's right. After all, they've been teaching us right from wrong all our lives. They might not like the way some of our friends look, but they should trust us to know what our friends are really like inside. My friend Jessica, for example, wears a lot of makeup. I know my parents don't like that, but Jessica is really OK inside.

(3)   Another reason for parents not to choose our friends is that we might not like the friends our parents want for us. We might find them boring. And we might have arguments with our parents about the people they choose.

(4)   Finally, if our parents want to give us advice about what friends to choose, they shouldn't do it without explaining themselves. They could say why they don't want us with a certain person. If they say why, then maybe we will understand. Maybe we will stop hanging out with that person if we know that what our parents tell us about him or her is true.

Score: _____

Reasons: _____

_____

_____

_____

DIRECTIONS: Read the following description of a writing task. Then read the two essays that were written on this topic.

When you have finished, give each essay a score and give your reasons. Then, working with a partner, tell why you gave each essay the score you did. Listen to the reasons your partner gave. Make any changes in scores and reasons that you wish.

> Write an essay for your principal discussing what might have caused students in your school to cheat on tests and relating what the results of their actions might be.

ESSAY 3

Dear Ms. _____:

(1) In this school there has been a big problem with the students. They have been cheating on tests and probraly even on classwork and homework.

(2) Most students cheat because when the teacher give a lesson they don't pay attention so they don't understand the work and then they have to take the test and they don't know the answers.

(3) Once we were taking a test and my friend wanted the answer. I told her no. Because I didn't want to get into troble. She got mad. I went to the bathroom, and she looked at my paper. I could tell because it was turned over. So I got mad and I told the teacher.

(4) The way to stop kids from cheating is to show them that its wrong and maybe give them a detention. Cheating is a stupid and idiotic thing to do, and there's a well known fact that it don't get you nowhere.

Score: _____

Reasons: _____

_____

_____

_____

ESSAY 4

Dear Ms._____:

(1)   Some students in our school have been caught cheating on tests and homework. There are many reasons that students cheat, but the main one is that cheating is easier than picking up a book and studying.

(2)   Often, students don't pay attention in class. Then after school they hardly bother to study. They would rather hang out with their friends instead of trying their best to do their work. The homework seems too hard to them, and it takes too much time, especially when they can just grab someone else's paper and copy it in 10 minutes.

(3)   If you haven't paid attention in class and you haven't done the homework, you don't know what you need to know to pass the tests. There's a lot of pressure to pass tests. Parents want their children to succeed. And kids don't want to fail and be left back. So students get desperate and copy off of someone else's paper in tests.

(4)   If you cheat, though, you can get into really big trouble. If you're caught, you get an F on the test. You also get reported to the principal and get a detention or suspension. Then you might be forced to go to summer school to make up the work you missed. All these things are worse than just not doing well on a test.

(5)   Finally, cheating might make you lazy. It's easier than studying, but then you never learn anything and you will have to keep on cheating. This can be a real problem when you're older and apply for a job. Some jobs have tests you have to take in order to get hired. If you've always depended on cheating, you might not be able to pass a test in this kind of situation. You can hurt yourself a lot by cheating.

Score: _____

Reasons: _____

_____

_____

_____

DIRECTIONS: Read the following description of a writing task. Then read the two essays that were written on this topic.

When you have finished, give each essay a score and give your reasons. Then, working with a partner, tell why you gave each essay the score you did. Listen to the reasons your partner gave. Make any changes in scores and reasons that you wish.

> Write a letter to the editor of the local newspaper offering suggestions to help solve the problem of the homeless in society or in your own community.

ESSAY 5

Dear Editor:

(1)   I wanted to tell you there is a big problem that no one hasn't done anything about. Their is a lot of homeless in the streets. They haven't got any food, and in my community there are hunderds of homeless with children.

(2)   We can solve this problem by building shelters and feeding the homeless. And giving them warm clothes. They also need a job and good health care. Babie's can die of hunger, and that shouldn't happen in a place like America.

(3)   If we don't have enough shelters, the homeless has no place to go and the streets are not safe. The children get killed when drug gangs have a shoot out and hit them by misteak.

(4)   How can we say we live in the best country in the world? When we treat our people like this? We give alot of money to help other people throughout the world. What are we doing about our children? I hope you will listen to me and take my suggestions about how to help the homeless.

Score: _____

Reasons: _____

_____

_____

_____

ESSAY 6

Dear Editor:

(1)   One of the biggest problems we have in America today is the problem of the homeless. People who lose their jobs soon run out of money. They have no food and no place to live.

(2)   Entire families are out on the street. Sometimes they spend the night in a shelter. Sometimes they live in a tent or a cardboard box. The children in these families never know where they are going to be from one day to the next. They don't have warm clothes or hot food. Most of the time they don't go to school. There is an old garage across from our school where the homeless people go on rainy days. I look at them and wonder why something can't be done.

(3)   To solve this problem we first have to take care of the people who are out on the street. There are lots of old buildings in this town that aren't being used. We could raise money to fix up those places and turn them into shelters where whole families could stay until they found another place to live. Supermarkets and restaurants could contribute leftover food, and students could volunteer to help in the kitchen. Children could go to the local school and get help with reading and math from more student volunteers.

(4)   Second, we have to help people help themselves. People who lose their jobs need to learn how to get new ones. They would get trained by local businesses and then have jobs. If they still didn't earn enough money to find a place of their own, they would get help with the rent and with food until they earned enough to take care of their families. Mothers would need day care centers that were safe so that they could leave their children there when they went to work.

(5)   Where would the money come from? We should use some of the money we spend on guns and bombs to help our families. After all, families are the future for America.

Score: _____

Reasons: _____

_____

_____

_____

Use the following chart as a guide when you write your own essays.

---

1. CONTENT

- State the central idea clearly.

- Use details, facts, and examples to support or elaborate the central idea.

- Make sure the support or elaboration is relevant and convincing.

- Keep the audience in mind.

2. ORGANIZATION

- Arrange ideas and facts in an order that is logical and appropriate.

- Make the order clear to the reader.

- Stick to the topic.

3. CONTROL OF LANGUAGE

- Make sure ideas are expressed clearly and connected logically.

- Use well-constructed sentences.

- Vary sentence structure and word choice.

- Avoid errors in usage, punctuation, and spelling.

---

3. WRITING ABOUT A CONTROVERSIAL ISSUE

A. CRITICAL THINKING: WAYS OF EXPRESSING AN OPINION

On the EWT test, you may be asked to write an essay expressing your opinion on a controversial issue.

A **controversial issue** is an issue that people disagree on. It can be personal, like "How late should I be allowed to stay out at night?" or it can be an issue that affects everybody, like "Who should be the next President?"

This chapter will give you practice in the thinking skills you need to write this kind of essay.

REACTING TO A CONTROVERSIAL ISSUE

Imagine you see this headline in your local newspaper:

> # SCHOOLS TO BE OPEN ALL YEAR!

Here are the reactions of two students. Which reaction is the most convincing?

Student 1: American students don't do as well as students from other countries. They need to go to school all year long.

Student 2: I don't want to go to school all year round. I think it's a stupid idea.

When asked for a reason, the second student replies:

Student 2: It's just stupid, that's all!

Is the response of the second student convincing? Would you be convinced by it?

OPINIONS, REASONS, FACTS, AND EXAMPLES

When you write an essay on a controversial issue, there is no "right" answer or "correct" opinion. What counts is your ability to back up your opinion with good reasons, facts, and examples.

- First, when you state your **opinion** on a controversial issue, you have to tell your reader what that opinion is. Some beginning writers forget to do this.

- Next, you need to give good **reasons** to support your opinion. The reasons tell your reader why you think the way you do.

- You also need **supporting facts** to make your reasons more believable to your reader. The more facts you have to support your reasons, the more your reader is inclined to agree with you.

- Finally, whenever you can, you should use **examples** from your own experience or the experience of others to show that your belief is based on real life.

Stating your opinion

What is this writer's opinion about a new state law requiring motorcycle riders to wear helmets?

> *I think everyone who rides a motorcycle should be required to wear a helmet.*

Giving a reason

You know that the writer agrees with the proposed new law, but you don't know why. If a friend said this to you, you could ask, "What makes you say that?" or "Why do you think so?" Then you would wait to hear the reasons.

Readers ask the same kinds of questions that listeners do, but they have no way of asking the writer. If you want to convince your reader, start by giving a reason that makes sense, as this writer did.

> I think everyone who rides a motorcycle should be required to wear a helmet **because helmets prevent head injuries.**

Supporting your reason with facts

Then the writer added a fact to elaborate the reason. When you **elaborate** an idea or a statement, you tell more about it. You give facts that support it, or you use more precise language to help your reader understand exactly what you are saying.

> I think everyone who rides a motorcycle should be required to wear a helmet because helmets prevent head injuries. **Head injuries are often very serious and can have long-term effects.**

Giving an example

Finally, to be even more convincing, the writer added an example drawn from personal experience.

> I think everyone who rides a motorcycle should be required to wear a helmet because helmets prevent head injuries. Head injuries are often serious and can have long-term effects. **Last spring, my friend Luis was riding behind his brother on their motorcycle. It was raining and they hit an oil patch and went out of control. Luis flew off the motorcycle and landed on his head. He was knocked unconscious and went into a coma.**

CHOOSING GOOD REASONS, FACTS, AND EXAMPLES

Reasons

Here are some of the ways we measure whether a reason is good.

1. It makes sense.

2. It is necessary. You have proved that you need it or that it needs to be done.

3. It doesn't cost much. What you suggest is either inexpensive or is worth what it costs.

4. It represents quality. Sports fans support the team they think is the best. Of course, they have to back up their opinion with facts when they talk to fans of other teams.

5. It gives pleasure. If you think something is worth doing because it's fun, that's OK.

6. It meets certain standards of ethics or personal values. You believe that certain things are right and certain things are wrong, and you base your opinions on those beliefs.

7. It has social value. Whatever you are suggesting is good or right for most people.

Discuss this list in class. Then add three more ways to describe a good reason.

8. _____

9. _____

10. _____

To state your reasons for disagreeing with something, just add **not** to the reasons above. (It does**n't** make sense; it is**n't** necessary, etc.)

✎ EXERCISE 1: DETERMINING GOOD REASONS

Rules are a part of everyone's life. There are school rules, family rules, and work rules. Choose one of these three sets of rules and write your choice here:

_____

Think about the individual rules in that set. Is there any one you find particularly hard to follow? Would you like to change it? Write the rule you would like to change in the space below:

_____

_____

Now comes the hard part. First, take a look at the list of ways to measure a good reason on pages 21-22. See if you can find two good reasons to change the rule you don't like. Write your reasons in the space below. When you write each of your reasons, start with its number on the chart. Don't forget to look at the ones you added.

Be prepared to explain your reasons in class.

_____

_____

Facts

You can begin a persuasive essay with two sentences like these:

> I think that our state should pass a law requiring everyone who rides a motorcycle to wear a helmet. ***First of all, statistics show that this state has more motorcycle accidents than any other state.***

In this example, the first sentence states your opinion, and the second sentence states a fact that supports your position. Your readers will take you seriously because you have given them a fact to support your opinion.

Here's another way to begin the essay.

> I think that our state should pass a law requiring everyone who rides a motorcycle to wear a helmet. ***If every rider wore a helmet, our state would be the safest in the country.***

In this example, the second sentence doesn't give a real fact. It just gives another opinion. A word like safest makes an alert reader ask questions: How do you measure safety? How can you be sure wearing a helmet would make our state "safest"? What proof do you have?

What is the difference between a fact and an opinion? The most important difference is this:

Facts can be checked. You can look them up in a reference book like a dictionary or an encyclopedia. Or you can call an expert. For example, if the fact you want to know is the number of accidents your state had last year, you can call the state Department of Transportation.

Facts come in many sizes, shapes, and colors. Facts can be about—

- *Chemical formulas*—The formula for water is H_2O.

- *Population figures*—There are 200 million people in the United States.

- *Names*—Marie Curie discovered radium.

- *Dates*—The Bill of Rights became part of the Constitution in 1791.

- *Sizes*—Grizzly bears weigh up to 1000 pounds.

- *Shapes*—A square has four equal sides.

- *Colors*—The colors in the rainbow are red, orange, yellow, green, blue, and violet.

Opinions cannot be checked. They are statements of belief. When someone writes a sentence like " Summer is my favorite time of year," you accept that statement as the writer's personal opinion. You don't question it, but you might expect to read some of the reasons why the writer thinks so.

When you read a sentence like "Sue Quarles is the ***best*** basketball player on our school team," you probably won't accept the statement without questioning it. You expect the writer to use statistics—how many goals Quarles has scored—or examples—spectacular plays Quarles has made against tough opponents—to prove the point.

A believable opinion is based on fact. Be prepared to provide some solid proof based on facts and believable examples when you use words like the following in your opinion essay:

> ***good, better, best, worst, most, least, easy, difficult***
>
> ***I think, feel, believe***
>
> ***always, never, none, all***

✎ EXERCISE 2: DISTINGUISHING FACT AND OPINION

Which statements below contain ***facts*** that can be checked? Write CHECK beside them.

Which statements are ***opinions*** that need to be supported by facts? Write PROOF beside them.

Be prepared to explain your choices.

1. Motorcycles are dangerous. _____

2. There were 150 motorcycle accidents in this state last year. _____

3. Congress should pass a new gun control law. _____

4. No smoking is allowed on any domestic airline flights. _____

5. Students who miss school can never learn enough to pass the exams. _____

6. The National Rifle Association (NRA) pays for ads to fight gun control laws. _____

7. I plan to take a course in word processing before I graduate. _____

8. Forty per cent of the survivors of motorcycle accidents suffer serious head wounds. _____

9. The best grilled chicken sandwich for your Busy Family is at your local B-Z Family Chicken Hut. _____

10. Today's B-Z Family Meal package is only $4.95 if you buy a portion of our new Sweet Tooth Fruit Salad. _____

11. Smoking makes some people cough. _____

12. A winning football team creates school pride. _____

13. Students who miss school must make up all their work within a week. _____

14. Working as a volunteer in a children's hospital is one of the most satisfying things I have ever done. _____

15. Our school cafeteria needs a new menu. _____

16. Showing community spirit through active volunteer work is part of the East Side High School tradition. _____

17. Yesterday only fourteen students ate the steamed cabbage that was part of the regular lunch. _____

18. More people eat in fast food restaurants than in regular restaurants. _____

19. America's favorite place to dine out with the family is in the local fast food restaurant. _____

20. Our district's school uniform consists of pants, shirt, and tie for the young men and plaid skirt, white blouse and jacket for the young women. _____

21. Students who wear uniforms pay more attention in class and are more serious about their work. _____

22. Taking extra courses in summer school is not a good idea because students need time off to be themselves without any pressure from teachers. _____

23. Last summer, 25% of this year's senior class took summer courses in SAT Prep. _____

24. Seniors improved their SAT scores by 75 points over the scores they got in their junior year. _____

25. Summer courses in SAT prep are a good way to improve your SAT score. _____

Examples

When you use your own experience or the experience of others as an example, be sure that the incident you have chosen relates directly to the point you are trying to make. Choosing **relevant** examples is an important strategy in presenting a convincing argument. Using an irrelevant example confuses your reader.

Here is a selection that you read earlier. Pay special attention to the paragraph in italics:

> I think everyone who rides a motorcycle should be required to wear a helmet because helmets prevent head injuries. Head injuries are often very serious and can have long-term effects. Last spring, my friend Luis was riding behind his brother on their motorcycle.
>
> *It was raining and they hit an oil patch and went out of control. Luis flew off the motorcycle and landed on his head. He was knocked unconscious and went into a coma.*

What if the writer had written this instead?

> I think everyone who rides a motorcycle should be required to wear a helmet because helmets prevent head injuries. Head injuries are often very serious and can have long-term effects. Last spring, my friend Luis was riding behind his brother on their motorcycle.
>
> *They had an accident and Luis landed on his head and broke his collarbone. The break was so bad that he couldn't play football this season, and now it looks like he won't get that athletic scholarship he was counting on.*

Which was worse for Luis—the head injury or the broken collarbone? Since the writer spends more time talking about the effects of the broken collarbone, the reader believes that the head injury was less serious. The example chosen does not show the importance of wearing helmets while riding a motorcycle. The writer should find another example, or should emphasize the seriousness of the head injury.

✎ *EXERCISE 3: CHOOSING RELEVANT EXAMPLES*

Think about the rules you decided to change in the last exercise. Using your own experience, describe an incident which serves as a good example of the reason you want to change the rule. Then tell your story to a classmate and ask if the example seems relevant.

Look out for one common trap in your writing! When you feel deeply about something, it is easy to exaggerate. One way of exaggerating is to jump to conclusions on the basis of one or two examples. Here is how one writer expressed her fear of the power of advertising:

> Advertising makes young people want things they can't afford or that aren't good for them. They make expensive sneakers so popular that young people rob and kill to get them. These kinds of ads should be stopped.

Do you really believe the writer, or do you think that she has overstated her case?

✎ EXERCISE 4: FINDING EXAGGERATED STATEMENTS

Discuss in class the paragraph above about advertising and expensive sneakers, using the following points to guide you.

- Is the first sentence entirely true? Does advertising always do this?

- Is the second sentence true all of the time, some of the time, once in a while, or not at all?

- Do you agree with the last sentence? What does the writer mean by "these kinds of ads"? Does anyone have the right to stop ads?

In the space below, write the conclusion you came to after the discussion about the paragraph.

_____

_____

_____

✎ *EXERCISE 5: IDENTIFYING AND REVISING EXAGGERATIONS*

Read the following statements. Identify any problems of exaggeration that you find. Discuss in class ways to revise the statements so that they are more effective and more believable.

1. Restaurants serve their customers too many fatty meals. If you want to live a long time, eat at home.

2. Today, being a good athlete gets you into a college on scholarship, but it doesn't help you get a degree. This is criminal, and athletes should refuse to play for teams that take advantage of them.

3. Schools should forbid students to work after school until senior year. My cousin Shivaun went to work in 9th grade and never graduated because she had no time to study.

3. WRITING ABOUT A CONTROVERSIAL ISSUE

B. WRITING YOUR ESSAY: A CONTROVERSIAL ISSUE ESSAY

This section will help you express your opinion on a controversial issue by—

- Showing you how to revise an unsuccessful essay

- Modeling the strategies used to write a successful essay

- Guiding you through the writing of your own essay

Here is a writing task that asks you to write an essay about a controversial issue. In the section called "Directions for Writing," you are told to—

- Develop a clear position

- Support the position with reasons and evidence

- Be aware of the other side

- Convince your readers that your position is reasonable

WRITING TASK

Writing Situation

At lunch you hear two classmates, Joe and Chris, talking nearby.

Joe: My parents say I can't hang around with Scott anymore. But they can't tell me not to be friends with someone.

Chris: Maybe it's for your own good. Scott has some pretty rough friends, and he's older, too.

Joe: Even so, I have a right to decide who my friends are. Don't my parents trust me?

This conversation raises a question for you: Do parents have a right to say who their children can spend time with?

The teen magazine you read has a column called "Kids Sound Off." You decide to send a letter on this controversial issue. Do you think parents should have a right to make rules about who their children's friends can be? Think about this issue and decide how you feel about it.

Directions for Writing

Write a letter to "Kids Sound Off" stating your position on the issue of whether parents should say who their children can spend time with. Begin your letter **Dear Editor:** Develop a clear position, and support it with reasons and evidence. Your readers may have a different view; therefore, your position will need to be supported by more than a strong feeling. Try to convince your readers that your point of view is reasonable.

ANALYZING AN UNSUCCESSFUL ESSAY

Here is the essay one student wrote:

Dear Editor:

(1)   I feel parents shouldn't choose your friends. When your in eighth grade. Because eighth graders are at an age when they mature. We have a right to choose who we want to be freinds with.

(2)   Here are the reasons I think this way. First, eighth graders are at an age when they start to grow up and mature alot. Some eighth-grade boys are ready to start shaving. We should know who to choose to hang around with. We have a right to make our own decisions.

(3)   Second, eighth graders got a right to choose who they want to be friends with. Parents shouldn't try to pick kids friends because they might pick the wrong friend.

(4)   In conclusion, I really feel parents shouldn't choose your friends.

This essay did not receive a passing score. Can you tell why? Look at "What Test Graders Look For" on page 8. Then write one reason that you think this essay did not pass.

_____

_____

Improving the Essay

Here are some questions good writers ask themselves when they revise an essay like this one. Think about each question. Then in the blanks following the questions, write the changes you would make in this essay. Notice that you won't be changing grammar, spelling, or punctuation just yet.

1. What do the "Directions for Writing" ask the writer to do? Does the first paragraph of the essay state the issue? Does it state the writer's position? If not, what changes should you make?

   • Rewrite paragraph 1 here:

_____

_____

_____

_____

2. The body of the essay should support the writer's position with reasons, facts, and examples that will convince the reader. What reason does the writer give at the start of paragraph 2? Does the writer elaborate, or develop, this reason with facts or examples? If not, what changes should you make? Is there a sentence in this paragraph that does not stick to the topic?

   • Rewrite paragraph 2 here:

_____

_____

_____

_____

3. Each paragraph in the body of the essay should state and support a new reason. Which sentence in paragraph 3 gives a new reason? What facts or examples can you give to support this reason? Is there a sentence in paragraph 3 that is unnecessary because it repeats something that has already been said?

• Rewrite paragraph 3 here:

_____

_____

_____

_____

4. A good closing adds something new. Does the last sentence of this essay state something new? If not, what additional facts or examples can you give to improve the closing? (**HINT**: You will leave your readers with a good impression if you can give a supporting detail or an example that shows the benefits of your position.)

• Rewrite paragraph 4 here:

_____

_____

_____

_____

Checking for Mechanical Errors

There are 7 errors in punctuation, spelling, usage, and sentence construction in the original version of this essay. Go back to the original version and circle each error. Then re-read the revisions you have written. Correct any errors in punctuation, spelling, usage, and sentence construction you find there. If you need help, check "Skills and Practice," pages 123-42.

ANALYZING A SUCCESSFUL ESSAY

Here is an example of a successful essay—an essay that would receive a passing grade. This sample can serve as a model for organizing your own essay. In addition, when you analyze the model, you can find out what strategies the writer used to make the essay successful.

Dear Editor:

(1)   I am writing to you about the question of whether parents should say who their children can spend time with. As an eighth-grader, I think that teenagers should be allowed to choose their own friends. Even though we are still not adults and we don't always know who our real friends are, our parents should not tell us that we can't hang out with someone without explaining why.

(2)   Parents should trust us. They should know that we know what's wrong and what's right. After all, they've been teaching us right from wrong all our lives. They might not like the way some of our friends look, but they should trust us to know what our friends are really like inside. My friend Jessica, for example, wears a lot of makeup. I know my parents don't like that, but Jessica is really OK inside.

(3)   Another reason for parents not to choose our friends is that we might not like the friends our parents want for us. We might find them boring. And we might have arguments with our parents about the people they choose.

(4)   Finally, if our parents want to give us advice about what friends to choose, they shouldn't do it without explaining themselves. They could say why they don't want us with a certain person. If they say why, then maybe we will understand. Maybe we will stop hanging out with that person if we know that what our parents tell us about him or her is true.

Analyzing the Essay

Answer the following questions. They will help you find out what strategies the writer used to make this essay successful.

A. THE OPENING: PARAGRAPH 1

- Does the writer give you a clear idea of what the issue is and what the writer's position is?

  _____

- Does the essay have a strong opening?

  _____

The writer states the issue in the first sentence. In the second sentence, the writer makes his/her position clear. In addition, the writer adds strength to the opening by briefly stating one of the reasons that he/she feels this way. Indicating one of your reasons at the start helps you organize your thoughts and lets your readers know that you will be presenting a convincing argument.

B. THE BODY: PARAGRAPHS 2-4

- Does each paragraph discuss a different reason?

  _____

- Does the writer give enough details to support each of the reasons?

  _____

- Do the writer's reasons make sense?

  _____

- Will the writer's reasons appeal to the readers?

  _____

- Does the writer stick to the topic?

  _____

Content/Organization

Paragraphs 2-4 are the body of the essay. The writer's reasons for believing that eighth-graders should choose their own friends are developed in this part of the essay. In each paragraph of the body of this essay, the writer presents a different reason for the position he/she has taken. The rest of each paragraph contains the details supporting that reason. The writer sticks to the topic and uses words and phrases like "for example," "another reason" and "finally" to make transitions.

Although this writer gives three reasons, a successful essay can also have two reasons that are well developed. Notice that the writer chooses reasons that will convince the editor of "Kids Sound Off."

Writing Good Reasons

1. Choose reasons that you are able to support. For example, "Parents don't know anything about us" is a statement that is difficult to prove. If you choose a reason that is exaggerated and unrealistic, you will not be able to elaborate this part of your essay convincingly.

○ **STRATEGY: Jotting down ideas beforehand or writing an outline will help you discard reasons you can't support.**

2. Keep your audience in mind. Choose reasons that mean something to your audience.

○ **STRATEGY: To select the reasons that will appeal to your audience, try asking questions like the following:**

   • **Is it necessary?** Does it need to be done, or do you need it?

   • **Does it benefit anyone?** is it good for you or for someone else?

   • **Is the cost reasonable?** Is it worth it, not only in dollars but in time, effort, and so on?

   • **Is it important to your personal values?** Does it fit your own idea of what is right or good?

   • **Is it important for society?** Is it right or good for most people?

3. Remember to support your opinion with facts, examples, and other details. You don't need to avoid opinions; you just need to be able to tell the difference between an opinion and a fact. Avoid supporting an opinion with another opinion.

○ **STRATEGY: For each supporting statement, ask yourself, "Is this a fact or an opinion?"**

4. Let your readers know how strongly you feel about the subject, but don't exaggerate your feelings or use abusive language. Remember that persuasion means winning someone over, not beating someone over the head.

✪ *STRATEGY: Check your essay for words and phrases like "everyone always does . . .," "no one ever . . .," "stupid idea," "best," "worst," and "only." These may be indications of exaggerated language or abusive language.*

Usage/Sentence Construction/Mechanics

Throughout the essay, the structure of the sentences and the writer's choice of words is interesting and varied. The grammar, spelling, punctuation, and sentence construction are also correct.

C. THE CLOSING

- Does the essay have a strong closing?

To conclude the essay, this writer offers an alternative that both teenagers and parents might find appealing. This is an effective technique to use when you are taking a position on a controversial issue.

WRITING AND EVALUATING YOUR OWN ESSAY

Now you are going to write an essay of your own. Look at the following Writing Task:

WRITING TASK

Writing Situation

Accidents can have very serious consequences for bicycle riders. Wearing a safety helmet, however, reduces the possibility of brain injury by 90%. For this reason, the state of New Jersey has just passed a law stating that bicycle riders who are 13 years old or younger must wear safety helmets. Some people object to this law because the helmets are expensive and uncomfortable.

What do you think about this law? Is it a good law, or do you think it should be changed?

Directions for Writing

Write a letter to the editor of your local newspaper stating your position on the issue of whether bicycle riders up to the age of 13 should be required to wear safety helmets. Begin your letter **Dear Editor:** State your position clearly and support it with reasons, facts, and examples. Remember to convince your readers that your point of view is reasonable.

Reading the Description of the Writing Task

This strategy will help you understand the writing task, find out how you feel about the issue, and begin to organize your ideas.

Read the questions below. Then write your answers to each one.

STEP 1: READ THE DESCRIPTION OF THE WRITING TASK

How do I feel about this question/situation? What is my position?

_____

_____

STEP 2: IDENTIFY THE TASK

What am I supposed to do?

- What question/issue am I supposed to address? _____

_____

- What is the purpose of my essay? _____

_____

- Who is my audience? _____

_____

STEP 3: READ BETWEEN THE LINES

What other facts might I need to answer this question? (For example, do I need to know why brain injury is more serious than other kinds of injury?)

_____

_____

STEP 4: USE PERSONAL EXPERIENCE

What do I know about this topic?

- Can I tell about an experience of my own? _____

  _____

- Can I tell about an experience someone else has had? _____

  _____

- Have I heard or read about this topic or seen something about it on TV?

  _____

  _____

STEP 5: FORM A FINAL OPINION

How do I feel about this question/issue now? _____

_____

Memorize these 5 steps. When you take the actual EWT, ask yourself these questions. Use the box marked PREWRITING/ PLANNING SPACE in the test booklet to jot down your answers. (WARNING: Don't forget to transfer ALL your good ideas when you write your draft. The scorers will not read your planning notes.)

Mapping the Essay

When you have finished Step 5 above, you will have decided what your position is. You will also have begun to think about how to support your position.

On a separate sheet of paper, start planning your essay. Follow the instructions below, and use the chart that follows as a guide to your planning.

1. Under the head "Brainstorming," jot down as many reasons as you can think of that support the position you have taken. You can write just words or phrases instead of sentences.

2. Now evaluate your reasons. Are they sensible ones? Will they appeal to your audience? Can they be supported easily? Circle up to three reasons that you think will really persuade your readers.

3. In the box labeled "Body" on the chart, write every reason you circled above as a full sentence. (Remember that you need only two reasons if they are well developed.)

4. Beneath each sentence, under the head "Facts and Examples," jot down two or three facts or details that support the reason. (These do not have to be sentences.)

5. In the box headed "Opening" on the chart, state the issue and your position. Include any reasons that you can mention briefly in an opening.

6. If you have any special ideas about the closing of your essay, jot them down in the box headed "Closing." Remember that one possibility is to offer an alternative that will appeal to people on both sides of the issue. For an example, look at the last paragraph of the successful essay on page 33.

PERSUASIVE ESSAY

BRAINSTORMING

_____

_____

_____

OPENING

Issue: _____

Your Position: _____

BODY

Reason 1

_____

_____

_____

Facts & Examples

1. _____

2. _____

3. _____

Reason 2

_____

_____

_____

Facts & Examples

1. _____

2. _____

3. _____

Reason 3

_____

_____

_____

Facts & Examples

1. _____

2. _____

3. _____

CLOSING

_____

_____

_____

Writing the First Draft

Use what you have written in these mapping activities to write a first draft of your essay. Write your draft on a separate sheet of paper.

Evaluating and Improving the Essay

When you have finished your draft, read what you have written. Then use the following form to analyze your essay. Check the appropriate boxes, and jot down any comments you wish. You can work on your own or with a partner.

1. Does the essay give you a clear idea of what the issue is and what the writer's position is?

☐ yes   ☐ no   Comments:_____

2. Does the essay have a strong opening? For example, does the opening briefly mention a reason that will support the writer's position?

☐ yes   ☐ no   Comments:_____

3. Does each paragraph discuss a different reason?

☐ yes   ☐ no   Comments:_____

4. Does the writer give enough details to support each of the reasons?

☐ yes   ☐ no   Comments:_____

5. Do the writer's reasons make sense, and do they appeal to the reader?

☐ yes   ☐ no   Comments:_____

6. Does the writer stick to the topic?

☐ yes   ☐ no   Comments:_____

7. Does the writer use transitional words to connect paragraphs?

☐ yes   ☐ no   Comments:_____

8. Does the writer use interesting words and phrases?

☐ yes   ☐ no   Comments:_____

9. Does the writer use different types of sentences to make the essay interesting?

☐ yes   ☐ no   Comments:_____

10. Does the essay have a strong closing? For example, does it offer an appealing alternative?

☐ yes   ☐ no   Comments:_____

Decide what changes would improve your essay, and make these changes on your paper. Remember that these sorts of improvements can make a difference in your test score.

For extra practice, make a final copy of your revised essay. This time, proofread it carefully and make sure that the grammar, punctuation, and spelling are all correct.

THINKING ABOUT CONTROVERSIAL ISSUES

What issues will you be asked to write about on the EWT?

Only the test makers know. But you can be sure that the test makers will expect you to be concerned about issues that other eighth graders feel deeply about.

If you want to find out what other eighth graders think is important, take a survey in class. Answer the following questions:

> What do I argue with my parents about?

> What do I worry about in my community?

> What do my friends talk about?

> Are there things I'm not allowed to do that I feel I should do?

> Are there rules at school I'd like to change?

Spend some time each week talking over the list of issues that mean a lot to your and your class. Add to the list when something happens. Discussing issues openly and honestly will help prepare you for the EWT.

4. WRITING ABOUT CAUSES AND EFFECTS

A. CRITICAL THINKING: UNDERSTANDING CAUSES AND EFFECTS

In the first section of this book, you learned how to write an essay that gives your opinion on a controversial issue.

A second kind of essay you may have to write for the EWT is one in which you discuss *causes and effects*.

This chapter will give you practice in the thinking skills you need to write this kind of essay.

IDENTIFYING CAUSES AND EFFECTS

Why does a baby cry? Often, the *cause* is that it's hungry.

What happens when a hungry baby cries? Usually, the *effect* of its crying is that someone picks the baby up and feeds it.

Many events or actions have this sort of cause-effect relationship. One thing causes another to happen. Or something happens as the result of something else. We deal with causes and effects every day when we ask questions like—

- *Why* did that happen? *(The speaker is looking for a cause.)*

- *What is the reason* for that? *(The speaker is looking for a cause.)*

- *What happened* when he said that? *(The speaker is looking for an effect.)*

- What was the *result*? *(The speaker is looking for an effect.)*

How do you explain what might have caused something to happen? How do you explain what the consequences (or effects) of a particular action or decision might be? You'll need to rely on critical thinking skills like the following:

- Using common sense to make reasonable guesses about why particular things happen or about the consequences of decisions, actions, or events.

- Recognizing that an effect may also be the cause of something.

- Distinguishing cause-effect relationships from other kinds of relationships, such as problem-solution.

USING COMMON SENSE

Imagine this. At 8:00 on a Wednesday morning, as people are leaving their homes for work, it starts to pour. Immediately, nearly all the people turn around and go back into their houses. Why?

- Because they have remembered phone calls they need to make?

- Because they have decided to stay home all day?

- Because they want to get umbrellas they have in their homes?

It's possible that one or two of these people might have a phone call to make. It's even possible that someone might end up staying home. But common sense helps you come to the conclusion that all these people are going back for umbrellas. This is the most reasonable explanation of their action.

When you speculate about causes and effects, common sense should be your guide. The most reasonable explanation of why something happened is usually the most convincing. In the same way, when you draw conclusions about the possible consequences of an action, you look for an explanation that is logical and reasonable.

✎ EXERCISE 1: USING COMMON SENSE IN IDENTIFYING CAUSES

Choose the sentence (A, B, or C) that makes the most sense in the blank. Remember to use common sense; look for reasonable answers to the question "Why?"

1. Kim, Jessica, and Erika are good friends. Maria wants to sit with them at lunch and spend time with them after school. _____. So Maria walks off by herself with tears in her eyes.

   A. Kim, Jessica, and Erika tell Maria how much they like her and invite her to sit with them.

   B. Kim, Jessica, and Erika ignore Maria and don't make room for her at their lunch table.

   C. Kim, Jessica, and Erika kick Maria, spit on her, and call her terrible names.

44

2. Anyone who is caught fighting on school property gets an automatic suspension. _____. So when the principal comes out to see what's happening, Chuck runs away.

   A. Chuck gets into a fight with Richard in the school yard.

   B. Chuck see two friends of his fighting in the lunchroom.

   C. Chuck and a friend get into a fight on their way to school.

3. Nicole's father died when she was young, and her mother doesn't make much money. _____. So she baby-sits every weekend and two afternoons during the week.

   A. Nicole wants to learn how to take care of young children.

   B. Nicole wants to be a billionaire by the time she is 25.

   C. Nicole wants to buy an expensive dress for the graduation party.

✎ EXERCISE 2: USING COMMON SENSE IN IDENTIFYING EFFECTS

Choose the sentence (A, B, or C) that makes the most sense in the blank. Remember to use common sense when you answer the question "What might happen next?" Avoid explanations that are exaggerated or improbable. Instead, think about what is most likely to happen.

1. If the hole in the ozone layer gets larger, more humans will develop skin cancer. Recently, there has been an increase in the kind of pollution that destroys the ozone layer. _____.

   A. Skin cancer can be expected to increase.

   B. Millions of people will die of skin cancer.

   C. Cancer will no longer be a major problem.

2. Gerard spent spring vacation visiting his Uncle Leonard in Florida. When he got home, Gerard wrote to his uncle, thanking him for a great time. _____.

   A. Uncle Leonard put the letter aside and forgot to read it.

   B. Uncle Leonard was pleased and decided to invite Gerard again.

   C. Gerard was annoyed at having to write his uncle a letter.

45

3. Rose's family came to this country less than a year ago. Rose couldn't speak any English. _____.

   A. The principal would not let Rose go to our school.

   B. Rose took a special class in English at our school.

   C. Rose taught everyone her language and never learned English.

AN EFFECT CAN ALSO BE THE CAUSE OF SOMETHING

When you explain cause-effect relationships, watch out. The result of one event might at the same time be the cause of another. For example, George Power's voice is very loud. When he's on the phone, his daughter Julia turns up the volume on the TV. Why? Because George's voice is so loud that she can't hear the TV. But then George raises his voice so that the TV won't drown him out. What's the result? Julia turns up the TV even more.

✎ EXERCISE 3: FINDING CAUSES AND EFFECTS

What are the causes in the paragraph below? What are the effects? Which things are both cause and effect?

> On the side of a mountain, bare rocks are often exposed to the weather. Wind and ice dig out bits of the rocks, and dirt is able to accumulate in the cracks. Mosses and grasses, and eventually small shrubs, can take root in this dirt. The plants grow and shed their leaves, which decay and add another layer to the soil. After a while, the soil is deep enough and rich enough for trees to sprout where there once was only rock.

DISTINGUISHING CAUSE-EFFECT FROM PROBLEM-SOLUTION

Sometimes, when you are writing about causes and effects, you accidentally slip into the language of a problem-solution essay. This can happen especially easily when you are discussing the causes and effects of a situation that is also a problem—for example, cheating in school.

Remember that your job in a cause-effect essay is just to explain—to answer the questions "For what reason?" and "What will happen as a result?" In a cause-effect essay, you are NOT writing about a possible solution of a problem.

Here is an example:

> Oliver cheated on his math test. What might happen as a consequence?

Here are possible answers:

> A. Oliver will get caught and be given detention.
>
> B. Oliver will become a criminal and go to jail.
>
> C. Oliver should be put in a room by himself during tests.

Choices A and B both describe things that might happen in the future, although Choice A is clearly more reasonable and probable than Choice B. The verbs ("will get caught"; "will become") tell you that these sentences are about future events.

Choice C, however, does not speculate about the consequences, or effects, of Oliver's cheating. Instead, it offers a solution to the problem of his cheating. The verb "should" is a clue that the writer has begun to talk about solving problems.

✎EXERCISE 4: EXPLAINING EFFECTS INSTEAD OF PROPOSING SOLUTIONS

In each of the following situations, one answer choice is a *probable effect,* one is an *improbable effect,* and one is a *proposed solution.*

Choose the answer (A, B, or C) that makes the most sense in the blank. Remember that your answer should be a statement about the probable effects, NOT a recommendation for a way to solve a problem.

1. Last night Angela studied very hard for the spelling test because spelling is her poorest subject.

   A. Today Angela decided not to go to school at all.

   B. The teacher should give Angela extra help with spelling.

   C. Angela answered every question on the test correctly.

2. Brookfield School has decided that students should help take care of the school. Someone has painted graffiti on all the first-floor windows.

   A. During their lunch hour, teams of students will clean the first-floor windows.

   B. The students who painted the graffiti will be given an award for making the school more beautiful.

   C. The school should hire more security guards to keep people from doing things like this.

3. Rodney's father doesn't like the way Rodney dresses. Rodney is about to leave for school in pants turned inside out and a T-shirt with torn-off sleeves.

   A. Rodney should try to have a talk with his father about the way he dresses.

   B. Rodney's father will look upset and say, "How can you go out looking like that?"

   C. Rodney's father will admire the way he is dressed and ask whether he can borrow a shirt.

4. WRITING ABOUT CAUSES AND EFFECTS

B. WRITING YOUR ESSAY: A CAUSE / EFFECT ESSAY

In an essay that speculates about causes and effects, you usually explain what causes something to happen. You also explain what the results, or consequences, might be.

This section will help you write about causes and effects by—

- Showing you how to revise an unsuccessful essay

- Modeling the strategies used to write a successful essay

- Guiding you through the writing of your own essay

Here is a writing task that asks you to write a cause-effect essay:

WRITING TASK

Writing Situation

Some students in your school have been caught cheating. During tests they have copied answers from other students' papers. The principal has asked all the eighth-graders to write an essay that will help her understand the situation. You decide to write an essay about what caused these students to cheat and what the effects of their cheating might be.

Directions for Writing

Write an essay for your principal discussing what might have caused students in your school to cheat on tests and relating what the results of their actions might be. Be specific about both the causes and the effects. What are some reasons students might cheat? What exactly could happen as the result of cheating?

ANALYZING AN UNSUCCESSFUL ESSAY

Here is the essay one student wrote:

Dear Ms. _____:

(1)   In this school there has been a big problem with the students. They have been cheating on tests and probably even on class work and homework.

(2)   Most students cheat because when the teacher give a lesson they don't pay attention so they don't understand the work and then they have to take the test and they don't know the answers.

(3)   Once we were taking a test and my friend wanted the answer. I told her no. Because I didn't want to get into troble. She got mad. I went to the bathroom, and she looked at my paper. I could tell because it was turned over. So I got mad and I told the teacher.

(4)   The way to stop kids from cheating is to show them that its wrong and maybe give them a detention. Cheating is a stupid and idiotic thing to do, and there's a well known fact that it don't get you nowhere.

This essay did not receive a passing score. Can you tell why? Look at "What Test Graders Look For" on page 8. Then write one reason that you think this essay did not pass.

_____

_____

Improving the Essay

Here are some questions good writers ask themselves when they revise an essay like this one. Think about each question. Then in the blanks following the questions, write the changes you would make in this essay. Notice that you won't be changing grammar, spelling, or punctuation just yet.

1. What do the "Directions for Writing" ask the writer to do? In the first paragraph, does the writer state the purpose of this essay? If not, what changes should you make?

50

- Rewrite paragraph 1 here.

_____

_____

_____

_____

2. What cause of cheating does the writer discuss in paragraph 2? Does this seem like a reasonable explanation? Does the writer use facts or examples to help make this explanation convincing?

3. Does the writer give any other causes of cheating? If not, what are some additional causes this writer could discuss? What specific facts or examples could you give to make each cause believable?

4. Does the example in paragraph 3 tell you anything about the causes of cheating? Does it explain the effects of cheating? Is this paragraph unnecessary?

- Rewrite paragraphs 2 and 3 here as one paragraph about the causes of cheating. Include supporting details, facts, and examples. Be as specific as you can:

_____

_____

_____

_____

_____

_____

_____

_____

5. The body of the essay should discuss both causes and effects. Does paragraph 4 explain the effects of cheating? If not, what does the writer do in paragraph 4? Do these ideas belong in a cause-effect essay?

6. Is the language of the last sentence in this paragraph reasonable? If not, how could you change it?

- Write a new paragraph 3 that discusses the possible effects of cheating. Include supporting details, facts, and examples. Be as specific as you can:

_____

_____

_____

_____

_____

_____

_____

7. A good closing adds a new fact or idea to your explanation. What additional ideas can you give to conclude the essay? (Remember that you are discussing causes and effects, NOT offering solutions to a problem.)

- Write a new paragraph 4 here:

_____

_____

_____

_____

Checking for Mechanical Errors

There are 7 errors in punctuation, spelling, usage, and sentence construction in the original version of this essay. Go back to the original version and circle each error. Then re-read the revisions you have written. Correct any errors in punctuation, spelling, usage, and sentence construction you find there. If you need help, check "Skills and Practice," pages 124-42.

ANALYZING A SUCCESSFUL ESSAY

Here is an example of a successful essay—an essay that would receive a passing grade. This sample can serve as a model for organizing your own essay. In addition, when you analyze the model, you can find out what strategies the writer used to make the essay successful.

Dear Ms. _____ :

(1)   Some students in our school have been caught cheating on tests and homework. There are many reasons that students cheat, but the main one is that cheating is easier than picking up a book and studying.

(2)   Often, students don't pay attention in class. Then after school they hardly bother to study. They would rather hang out with their friends instead of trying their best to do their work. The homework seems too hard to them, and it takes too much time, especially when they can just grab someone else's paper and copy it in 10 minutes.

(3)   If you haven't paid attention in class and you haven't done the homework, you don't know what you need to know to pass the tests. There's a lot of pressure to pass tests. Parents want their children to succeed. And kids don't want to fail and be left back. So students get desperate and copy off of someone else's paper in tests.

(4)   If you cheat, though, you can get into really big trouble. If you're caught, you get an F on the test. You also get reported to the principal and get a detention or suspension. Then you might be forced to go to summer school to make up the work you missed. All these things are worse than just not doing well on a test.

(5)   Finally, cheating might make you lazy. It's easier than studying, but then you never learn anything and you will have to keep on cheating. This can be a real problem when you're older and apply for a job. Some jobs have tests you have to take in order to get hired. If you've always depended on cheating, you might not be able to pass a test in this kind of situation. You can hurt yourself a lot by cheating.

Analyzing the Essay

Answer the following questions. They will help you find out what strategies the writer used to make this essay successful.

A. THE OPENING: PARAGRAPH 1

- Does the writer give you a clear idea of what the topic is?

The writer states the topic in the first sentence. The second sentence introduces the first question the writer will answer: What causes students to cheat? This sentence also provides a transition to the next paragraph.

B. THE BODY: PARAGRAPHS 2-5

- In which paragraphs does the writer discuss the causes of cheating—the reasons that students cheat?

_____

- In which paragraphs does the writer discuss the effects of cheating—the things that can happen as a result of cheating?

_____

- Does the writer give enough specific details to explain why students cheat?

_____

- Does the writer give enough specific details to explain the effects of cheating?

_____

- Do the writer's explanations seem reasonable and convincing?

_____

- Are the writer's explanations arranged in an order that makes sense?

_____

- Does the writer stick to the topic?

_____

Content/Organization

Paragraphs 2-5 are the body of the essay. In paragraphs 2 and 3, the writer discusses the causes of cheating, explaining why students cheat on tests. In paragraph 4 and 5, the writer discusses the effects of cheating, explaining what could happen as a result of cheating.

Each paragraph contains one main idea and specific details that develop this idea. In the choice of details, the writer shows that he/she remembers the purpose of this paper: to help the principal understand the situation in their school. The writer also sticks to the topic and uses transition words like "if," "then," and "finally."

This writer has four paragraphs in the body of the essay, but a successful essay could have just two paragraphs in the body. The important thing is to keep the causes and effects separate. Discuss all the causes together in one or two paragraphs, then all the effects.

To provide convincing details, think of real-life cases of cheating that you know about. Why did the student cheat? How was the student punished? What, reasonably, might the long-term consequences be? Use common sense when you elaborate.

Usage/Sentence Construction/Mechanics

Throughout the essay, the structure of the sentences and the writer's choice of words is interesting and varied. The grammar, spelling, punctuation, and sentence construction are also correct.

C. THE CLOSING

- Does the writer make a strong closing statement?

_____

- Is the closing a separate paragraph?

_____

The closing of an essay doesn't have to be a separate paragraph. This writer's closing is one sentence—a general statement about the consequences of cheating that fits nicely at the end of paragraph 5. One interesting sentence makes a more effective closing than a paragraph that repeats ideas you've already stated.

WRITING AND EVALUATING YOUR OWN ESSAY

Now you are going to write an essay of your own. Look at the following Writing Task:

WRITING TASK

Writing Situation

   Two, three, or four people in a class often become very good friends. They hang out together in school and spend a lot of time with each other after school and on weekends. Usually it is difficult for a new person to join a group like this. Sometimes the group will even turn against one of its members. No one in the group will talk to the person who has been excluded; no one will spend time with this person.

   What causes students to form groups of this kind? What effect does a group like this have on the group members? What effect does it have on other students in the class?

Directions for Writing

   In your social studies class, you have been discussing cliques—groups of people who are very close and who exclude others. Write a paper for your teacher in which you explain very specifically why you think students in your school form cliques and what happens as a result.

Reading the Description of the Writing Task

This strategy will help you understand the writing task, find out how you feel about the issue, and begin to organize your ideas.

STEP 1: READ THE DESCRIPTION OF THE WRITING TASK

How might I answer this question? How could I explain this situation?

STEP 2: IDENTIFY THE TASK

What am I supposed to do?

- What question/issue am I supposed to address?

  _____

- What is the purpose of my essay?

  _____

- Who is my audience?

  _____

STEP 3: READ BETWEEN THE LINES

What other facts or examples might I need to answer this question? (For example, do I need to know how people feel when they are left out of a group?)

STEP 4: USE PERSONAL EXPERIENCE

What do I know about this topic?

- Can I tell about an experience of my own?

  _____

- Can I tell about an experience someone else has had?

  _____

- Have I heard or read about this topic or seen something about it on TV?

  _____

STEP 5: FORM A FINAL OPINION

How might I answer this question/explain this situation now?

_____

_____

Memorize these 5 steps. When you take the actual EWT, ask yourself these questions. Use the box marked PREWRITING/PLANNING SPACE in the test booklet to jot down your answers. (WARNING: Don't forget to transfer ALL your good ideas when you write your draft. The scorers will not read your planning notes.)

Mapping the Essay

When you have finished Step 5, above, you will have decided what causes and effects to discuss. You will have also begun to think about what details you can use to elaborate your explanation.

On a separate sheet of paper, start planning your essay. Follow the instructions below, and use the chart that follows as a guide to your planning.

1. Under the head "Causes," list as many reasons as you can think of why students form cliques. You can write just words or phrases instead of sentences.

2. Under the head "Effects," list as many of the effects as you can of this sort of behavior. Think about both the effects on the students in the clique and the effects on the students who are excluded. Again, you can use words or phrases instead of sentences.

3. Now evaluate the causes you have listed. Do they make sense? Are they reasonable explanations? Can you develop them with specific facts and examples? Circle each cause that is logical and reasonable and that you are sure you can develop.

   Under the head "Elaboration," list the facts, details, and examples you can use to develop the causes you have listed.

   The part of your essay that discusses the causes can be either one or two paragraphs.

4. Evaluate the effects in the same way. Do they seem reasonable and logical? Can you develop them with specific facts and examples? Circle each effect that makes sense and that you can develop.

   Then under the head "Elaboration," list the facts, details, and examples you can use to develop the effects you have circled.

   The part of your essay that discusses the effects can be either one or two paragraphs.

5. In the box headed "Opening" on the chart, state the situation and give the first reason you plan to explain.

6. If you have any special ideas about the closing of your essay, jot them down in the box headed "Closing." Remember that one possibility is to make a general statement about the consequences of forming cliques.

SPECULATING ABOUT CAUSES AND EFFECTS

OPENING

Question/Situation: _____

_____

A possible cause: _____

_____

BODY

Cause 1

_____

_____

Elaboration

_____

_____

Cause 2

_____

_____

Elaboration

_____

_____

Cause 3

_____

_____

Elaboration

_____

_____

Effect 1

_____

_____

Elaboration

_____

_____

Effect 2

_____

_____

Elaboration

_____

_____

Effect 3

_____

_____

Elaboration

_____

_____

CLOSING

_____

_____

_____

Writing the First Draft

Use what you have written in these mapping activities to write a first draft of your essay. Write your draft on a separate sheet of paper.

Evaluating and Improving the Essay

When you have finished your draft, read what you have written. Then use the following form to analyze your essay. Check the appropriate boxes, and jot down any comments you wish. You can work on your own or with a partner.

1. Does the essay give you a clear idea of what the question or situation is?

    ☐ yes   ☐ no   Comments:_____

2. Does the essay have a strong opening? For example, does the opening state one of the causes that the writer will discuss in this essay?

    ☐ yes   ☐ no   Comments:_____

3. Does the writer discuss all the causes together in one or two paragraphs and all the effects in another paragraph or two?

    ☐ yes   ☐ no   Comments:_____

4. Are these causes and effects logical and reasonable?

    ☐ yes   ☐ no   Comments:_____

5. Does the writer give enough details, facts, and examples to explain each of the causes and effects?

    ☐ yes   ☐ no   Comments:_____

6. Does the writer stick to the topic?

    ☐ yes   ☐ no   Comments:_____

7. Does the writer use transitional words to connect paragraphs and ideas within paragraphs?

    ☐ yes   ☐ no   Comments:_____

8. Does the writer use interesting words and phrases?

    ☐ yes   ☐ no   Comments:_____

9. Does the writer use different types of sentences to make the essay interesting?

    ☐ yes   ☐ no   Comments:_____

10. Does the essay have a strong closing? For example, does it make a general comment about the consequences of this situation?

☐ yes   ☐ no   Comments:_____

Decide what changes would improve your essay, and make these changes on your paper. Remember that these sorts of improvements can make a difference in your test score.

For extra practice, make a final copy of your revised essay. This time, proofread it carefully and make sure that the grammar, punctuation, and spelling are all correct.

THINKING ABOUT CAUSES AND EFFECTS

What causes and effects will you be asked to explain for the EWT?

You already know the answer to this question—only the testmakers know. But you practice this type of thinking whenever you ask yourself, "What would happen if I (didn't do any homework, lived 200 years in the future, etc.)?" or when you ask, "Why did this happen?"

Science and social studies classes are filled with questions about both cause and effect. Work with your classmates to make a list of questions that involve causes and effects in these subject areas. You can also practice this kind of thinking when you listen to the news on TV or radio. Ask yourself, "Why did this happen?" or "What will be the effect of this?"

Set aside some class time each week to discuss causes and effects that you hear about, read about, or learn about.

5. WRITING ABOUT THE SOLUTION TO A PROBLEM

A. CRITICAL THINKING: PROBLEM-SOLVING

In the first section of this book, you learned how to write an essay about a controversial issue and an essay about causes and effects.

The last kind of essay you may have to write for the EWT is one in which you offer a solution to a problem. This kind of essay is sometimes called a **problem-solution** essay.

This chapter will give you practice in the thinking skills you need to write this kind of essay.

IDENTIFYING AND DESCRIBING PROBLEMS

Everyone has problems. Here are some exercises that will help you solve some of yours.

✎ EXERCISE 1: WHAT ARE MY PROBLEMS?

Take five minutes and make a list of problems you have. Don't worry about whether someone else will think your problems are worth worrying about. They are important to you, and that's what counts.

The list can be as long or as short as you want, but be sure that you can understand it. For example, if you need money for a particular reason, don't just put down the word "money." Instead, also write what you need it for:

how to get money for CD player

Now you know that the problem is getting money and also what you want to use the money for once you get it.

Here is the list one student made. Use it to get ideas for your own list.

- getting along better with my parents
- finding time to do the homework I need to do

- finding time for rehearsing with my band

- I like shopping too much.

- losing my temper too often

- fighting with my brother

- peer pressure

✎ EXERCISE 2: WHICH PROBLEM SHALL I SOLVE FIRST?

Study the list you have made. Decide which problem you would like to tackle first, and write the number 1 beside it. Number the other items in the order of importance to you. Describe your Number 1 problem in a journal entry. You can begin this way:

My number 1 problem is _____

_____

_____

_____

_____

Tell who is involved in your problem, when it happens, what it involves, where it usually takes place, and why you think it happens.

Then write a sentence or two that explains why this problem is important to you:

_____

_____

COMING UP WITH SOLUTIONS THAT WORK

Do you have a friend you always tell your problems to? Does this friend come up with good solutions? Why do you like these solutions?

A good solution usually has three characteristics:

- It shows an understanding of the problem.

- It make sense—it solves the problem in a sensible way

- It can be done—it's practical, and nothing stands in the way.

Think about your number 1 problem. Is there any solution that comes first to your mind? Is this solution easy to put into practice? Do you really want to do it? You may want to talk over your problem with a friend or a relative.

✎ EXERCISE 3: MAKING A SOLUTION CHART

When you come up with a few ideas, write them in the chart below.
Then check off whether the solution makes sense and can be done.

	Solution	Makes sense	Can be done
1.	_____	_____	_____
2.	_____	_____	_____
3.	_____	_____	_____

COMPLICATED PROBLEMS

Finding a good solution to a complicated problem sometimes involves thinking about the consequences of each action you might take. (Remember, you worked with consequences when you worked with the cause-effect essay.)

Your friend Lara has a problem. When she was in a music store with her cousin last week, she saw her cousin put a tape in her pocket without paying for it. What should Lara do about this situation?

Your conversation goes something like this:

You: Tell her you don't want to go to the mall.

Lara: She'll want to know why.

You: Tell her you saw what she did.

Lara: She'll get mad.

You: Tell her you'll go but that you'll report her to the store manager if you see her take anything.

Lara: Maybe the manager will think I've been stealing too.

Every time you suggest something, Lara worries about its effects. This kind of reaction is normal. It is also a good way to anticipate further problems. You and Lara decide to make a chart showing what you have talked about and what is most likely to happen as the result of each action.

✎ EXERCISE 4: DETERMINING CONSEQUENCES

Complete the chart below, using the conversation between you and Lara as your source of information. Then add two new actions and their consequences.

Problem: What to do about shoplifting cousin

Action: Tell her you don't want to go to the mall.

Consequences: She'll want to know why.

Action: _____

Consequences: _____

Action: _____

Consequences: _____

Action: _____

Consequences: _____

Action: _____

Consequences: _____

✎ EXERCISE 5: SOLVING PROBLEMS

Read the situations below. Imagine that you are the one who has to make the decision. As you think about what you might do, make a chart that will show you the consequences of each step you consider taking.

1. You have different interests this year. Perhaps you have decided that you want to spend more time learning to play the guitar, or perhaps you really want to be good at a sport or a hobby. The friends you had last year aren't interested in anything new; they don't understand you. They don't want to be friends anymore. The other kids in class hang out in small groups. You would like to get to know them, but they don't seem to want to get to know new people. How can you make new friends?

2. You want to get a job babysitting, but your parents object. They want you to spend more time studying so that you can improve your grades. They also need you to help out more around the house, since they both work. You don't get much allowance, and you really want to start earning money to buy things you need. How can you satisfy them and get extra money at the same time?

3. You are worried about the state tests you will have to take in school this year. Everyone admits that they are difficult, but they also say that they are very important. Getting a good score means that you will be able to take the classes you want and that you won't have to take extra classes to catch up. What can you do to solve this problem?

AVOIDING EXAGGERATION

Sometimes you are so concerned about convincing your audience that some good action should be started or some bad action should be stopped that you exaggerate the effects of an action. For example, the world is struggling with the problems of pollution and the destruction of the environment. A student who feels deeply about this issue wants the school to do something to help the environment. She begins her essay this way.

> Our school can do something right now to save the planet. If we switch from using styrofoam cups in the cafeteria to regular glass, we can stop the hole in the ozone layer from getting any larger.

Is it really possible for the actions of one school to save the ozone layer? Probably not. Individual actions by themselves cannot solve an enormous problems. This paragraph needs revision. Here's a more convincing way of presenting the case.

> Our school can do something right now that will help us all learn to be more aware of our need to protect the atmosphere. If we switch from using styrofoam cups in the cafeteria to regular glass, we won't be adding to the problem. And we'll be educating students to be aware of the choices they must make.

✎ EXERCISE 6: UNDERSTANDING EFFECTIVE REVISION

Discuss the two paragraphs in class. Consider the following things:

- Look at the first sentence in each paragraph. Do they mean the same thing? Describe the difference in meaning in the space below.

_____

_____

- The second sentence in each paragraph begins the same way, but ends differently. Do you think the revision is more or less believable than the original? Write your response below.

_____

_____

- The writer added a sentence in revision. Does this sentence make the paragraph more or less believable? Write your response, with your reason.

_____

_____

USING FAIR LANGUAGE

To help you and your audience make a decision based on reason, it is important to use neutral language when you describe the issues that make up a problem. Using emotionally charged language (also called "loaded language") to present one side and not the other tells your reader which side you are on. It also suggests that you are unwilling to give your readers reasons that will let them make up their own minds.

✎ EXERCISE 7: USING NEUTRAL LANGUAGE

A. Read each statement and identify the issue. (Ask yourself: What is the subject of the discussion?) Can you tell which position the writer favors? Which words or phrases tell you this? Which statements are written in neutral language?

1. Any school which puts in a dress code for students is depriving them of their constitutional rights.

2. Some educators have reported that students who wear uniforms to school perform better on statewide tests and miss fewer days of school.

3. There is no question that the junk food consumed by many every day in fast food restaurants can lead to serious health problems.

4. A student who feels uncomfortable in school may find it hard to concentrate on learning.

5. Shorts and sandals belong on the beach, not in school.

6. Students have no right to demand that schools cater to every food whim.

7. As anyone who ever ate one knows, there is no such thing as a good school lunch.

8. Students have enough trouble passing courses they take for credit without having to worry about finding the time to do community service work for no pay and no grades.

9. Community services like the library, hospitals, playgrounds, and daycare centers couldn't do as much as they do without volunteer help.

10. Good nutrition, good value, and little waste is the goal of every school lunch program.

B. Rewrite five of the statements so that you cannot tell what the writer's position on the issue is.

1. _____

2. _____

3. _____

4. _____

5. _____

5. WRITING ABOUT THE SOLUTION TO A PROBLEM

B. WRITING YOUR ESSAY: A PROBLEM / SOLUTION ESSAY

When you write an essay that offers a solution to a problem, you begin by describing or explaining the problem so that your reader can become familiar with it. Then you offer one or two ways of solving the problem, making sure that your solutions make sense and seem reasonable.

This section will help you write about finding a solution to a problem by—

- Showing you how to revise an unsuccessful essay

- Modeling the strategies used to write a successful essay

- Guiding you in the writing of your own essay

Here is a writing task that asks you to write an essay that offers a solution to a problem.

WRITING TASK

Writing Situation

As a class assignment, you are to write a letter to the editor of the local newspaper about the problem of the homeless. Think about the problem. What are some suggestions that may help solve the problem of homeless people in society or even in your own community?

Directions for Writing

Write a letter to the editor of the local newspaper offering suggestions to help solve the problem of the homeless in society or in your own community. You will want to describe the problem so that your readers will understand how serious it is. Offer specific suggestions, and tell how these suggestions will help solve the problem. Convince your readers that your solution should be taken seriously. Use **Dear Editor:** to begin your letter.

ANALYZING AN UNSUCCESSFUL ESSAY

Here is the essay one student wrote:

Dear Editor:

(1)   I wanted to tell you there is a big problem that no one hasn't done anything about. Their is a lot of homeless in the streets. They haven't got any food, and in my community there are hunderds of homeless with children.

(2)   We can solve this problem by building shelters and feeding the homeless. And giving them warm clothes. They also need a job and good health care. Babie's can die of hunger, and that shouldn't happen in a place like America.

(3)   If we don't have enough shelters, the homeless has no place to go and the streets are not safe. The children get killed when drug gangs have a shoot out and hit them by misteak.

(4)   How can we say we live in the best country in the world? When we treat our people like this? We give alot of money to help other people throughout the world. What are we doing about our children? I hope you will listen to me and take my suggestions about how to help the homeless.

This essay did not receive a passing score. Can you tell why? Look at "What Test Graders Look For" on page 8. Then write one reason that you think this essay did not pass.

_____

_____

_____

_____

Improving the Essay

Here are some questions good writers ask themselves when they revise an essay like this one. Think about each question. Then in the blanks following the questions, write the changes you would make in this essay. Notice that you won't be changing grammar, spelling, or punctuation just yet.

1. What does the writing task ask the writer to do? In the first paragraph does the writer tell enough about the problem so that the reader has a general idea of what the essay is about? What changes should you make?

- Rewrite paragraph 1 here.

_____

_____

_____

_____

_____

_____

_____

2. Should paragraph 2 tell more about the problem or should it offer a solution?

- Rewrite the paragraph or write a new one.

_____

_____

_____

_____

_____

_____

_____

3. What solutions does the writer offer to solve this problem? What details, facts, and examples does the writer use to develop each solution? Does the writer indicate how each of the solutions could be achieved? What facts or examples could you give that would make each solution seem possible?

- Rewrite paragraph 2 so that each solution is developed by means of facts, examples, or details.

_____

_____

_____

_____

_____

_____

_____

_____

4. Does paragraph 3 help develop one of the solutions? If not, where should the content of this paragraph be placed?

_____

_____

5. Does this essay have a closing? Does it support one of the solutions or help the reader focus on the problem? Does the last sentence add anything to the essay?

- Rewrite paragraph 4 here.

_____

_____

_____

_____

_____

_____

_____

Checking for Mechanical Errors

There are 9 errors in punctuation, spelling, usage, and sentence construction in the original version of this essay. Go back to the original version and circle each error. Then re-read the revisions you have written. Correct any errors in punctuation, spelling, usage, and sentence construction you find there. If you need help, check "Skills and Practice," pages 124-42.

ANALYZING A SUCCESSFUL ESSAY

Here is an example of a successful essay—an essay that would receive a passing grade. This sample can serve as a model for organizing your own essay. In addition, when you analyze the model, you can find out what strategies the writer used to make the essay successful.

Dear Editor:

(1)   One of the biggest problems we have in America today is the problem of the homeless. People who lose their jobs soon run out of money. They have no food and no place to live.

(2)   Entire families are out on the street. Sometimes they spend the night in a shelter. Sometimes they live in a tent or a cardboard box. The children in these families never know where they are going to be from one day to the next. They don't have warm clothes or hot food. Most of the time they don't go to school. There is an old garage across from our school where the homeless people go on rainy days. I look at them and wonder why something can't be done.

(3)   To solve this problem we first have to take care of the people who are out on the street. There are lots of old buildings in this town that aren't being used. We could raise money to fix up those places and turn them into shelters where whole families could stay until they found another place to live. Supermarkets and restaurants could contribute leftover food, and students could volunteer to help in the kitchen. Children could go to the local school and get help with reading and math from more student volunteers.

(4)   Second, we have to help people help themselves. People who lose their jobs need to learn how to get new ones. They would get trained by local businesses and then have jobs. If they still didn't earn enough money to find a place of their own, they would get help with the rent and with food until they earned enough to take care of their families. Mothers would need day care centers that were safe so that they could leave their children there when they went to work.

(5)   Where would the money come from? We should use some of the money we spend on guns and bombs to help our families. After all, families are the future for America.

Analyzing the Essay

Answer the following questions. They will help you find out what strategies the writer used to make this essay successful.

A. THE OPENING: PARAGRAPH 1 AND 2

- Does the writer give you a clear idea of what the problem is and how serious the writer thinks it is?

  _____

- Does the essay have a strong opening?

  _____

The writer states the problem in the first sentence, and then elaborates it by describing how people become homeless. In the second paragraph the writer continues the development by adding specific details about what it is like to be homeless. It is clear that the writer uses details that he or she has really seen. The writer's feelings about the problem are made clear in the last sentence. It is important in any problem-solution essay to describe the problem as fully as you can before offering any solution. The more detailed you are, the more convinced your readers will be that you really know what you are talking about.

B. THE BODY: PARAGRAPHS 3-4

- Does each paragraph discuss a different part of the solution?

  _____

- Do the writer's suggestions make sense?

  _____

- Does the writer show how each suggestion could be carried out?

  _____

- Are the writer's suggestions practical?

  _____

- Does the writer stick to the topic?

Content/Organization

Paragraphs 2-4 are the body of the essay. Paragraph 2 gives the reader enough details to understand how important the problem is and states the writer's attitude toward the problem. In the third and fourth paragraphs, the writer focuses on two kinds of suggestions to overcome the problem. Paragraph 3 contains suggestions for solving the immediate problems of the homeless—food, clothing, shelter, schooling. Paragraph 4 suggests ways to solve the long-range problems—getting job training and receiving financial help. The writer sticks to the topic and use phrases like "we first have to" and "Second, we have to" to make transitions.

In addition to explaining the problem in detail, the writer offers practical solutions and makes suggestions that seem reasonable and do-able. A successful problem-solution essay should leave the reader with the feeling that something really can be done. Here are some tips to help you make practical suggestions.

1. Can you think of a specific way to get something done?

2. Have you thought about how much it will cost? How will it get paid for?

3. Does it take care of an important part of the problem?

4. Will someone be willing to do it?

5. Have you kept your audience in mind?

Usage/Sentence Construction/Mechanics

Throughout the essay, the structure of the sentences and the writer's choice of words is interesting and varied.

In the space below, copy two sentences you thought were particularly well written.

_____

_____

_____

_____

The grammar, spelling, and punctuation are also correct.

C. THE CLOSING

- Does the essay have a strong closing?

_____

The writer concludes strongly by asking where the money for these solutions will come from. The writer also answers the question by stating that saving families is at least as important as developing weapons. A closing does not have to be long to be convincing.

WRITING AND EVALUATING YOUR OWN ESSAY

Now you are going to write an essay of your own. Look at the following writing task.

WRITING TASK

Writing Situation

Families help each other out. Parents and grandparents help with homework; children do chores. Sometimes a mother has to go back to work when her child is too young for school. If she can't find good day care, she might ask her family to take turns caring for the baby. Your cousin Shara has been taking care of her aunt's baby every Wednesday after school and every Saturday morning. Now she has been chosen for a major part in the school's spring play. She doesn't want to disappoint her aunt, but she doesn't want to miss this opportunity.

She writes to you, asking for your help in solving this problem.

Directions for Writing

Write a letter to your cousin, advising her what to do about this problem. To let her know that you understand the situation, describe in your own words what the problem is and offer her at least two ways she can solve this problem. Give details to explain each solution fully, and make sure that your suggestions make sense and can be done. You can also make suggestions about the best way she can present her ideas to her family.

Reading the Description of the Writing Task

This strategy will help you understand the writing task, organize your ideas, and brainstorm some solutions.

STEP 1: READ THE DESCRIPTION OF THE WRITING TASK

Do I understand the problem? Do I understand both Shara's point of view and her aunt's? What solution comes immediately to my mind?

_____

_____

_____

STEP 2: IDENTIFY THE TASK

What am I supposed to do?

- What problem am I supposed to find a solution for?

  _____

  _____

- What is the purpose of my essay?

  _____

  _____

- Who is my audience?

  _____

  _____

STEP 3: READ BETWEEN THE LINES

What other facts might I need to answer this question? (For example, do I need to know who takes care of the baby the other days of the week?)

_____

_____

_____

STEP 4: USE PERSONAL EXPERIENCE

What do I know about this kind of problem?

- Can I tell about an experience of my own?

  _____

- Can I tell about an experience someone else has had?

  _____

- Have I heard or read about this topic or seen something about it on TV?

  _____

STEP 5: FORM A FINAL OPINION

What solution do I think will work now?

_____

_____

_____

_____

_____

Memorize these 5 steps. When you take the actual EWT, ask yourself these question. Use the PREWRITING/PLANNING space in the test booklet to jot down your answers. (WARNING: Don't forget to transfer ALL your good ideas when you write your draft. The scorers will not read your planning notes.)

Mapping the Essay

When you have finished Step 5 above, you will have decided on one or more solutions. You will also have thought of experiences that you have had that can be used to explain why a solution makes sense. On a separate sheet of paper, start planning your essay. Follow the instructions below and use the chart on the next page as a guide to your planning.

1. Under the head "Opening," state the problem briefly as if you were explaining it to someone who doesn't know it.

2. Under the head, "Brainstorming," list as many solutions as you can think of that would solve the problem. At this stage don't worry about how workable these solutions are—just list them.

3. Now evaluate your solutions. Which ones make sense? Which ones are practical? Which ones are realistic? Which ones would please everyone involved? Write each workable solution in the box labeled "Body."

4. For each workable solution, think of a fact that you know or a situation you have experienced or heard about that could serve as an example. Jot it down under "Fact/Examples."

5. If you have any special ideas about the closing of your essay, jot them down in the box headed "Closing." A good way to end a letter that offers advice about solving a problem is to suggest how the person you're writing to can present the solution to the people involved.

PROBLEM/SOLUTION ESSAY

BRAINSTORMING

_____

_____

_____

OPENING:
DEFINING THE PROBLEM

_____

_____

BODY

Solution 1

_____

_____

_____

Fact/Examples

_____

_____

_____

Solution 2

_____

_____

_____

Fact/Examples

_____

_____

_____

CLOSING

_____

_____

_____

Writing the First Draft

Use what you have written in these mapping activities to write a first draft of your essay. Write your draft on a separate sheet of paper.

Evaluating and Improving the Essay

When you have finished your draft, read what you have written. Then use the following form to analyze your essay. Check the appropriate boxes, and jot down any comments you wish. You can work on your own or with a partner.

1. Does the essay give you a clear idea of what the problem is, how important it is, and how you propose to solve it?

☐ yes ☐ no   Comments:_____

2. Does the essay have a strong opening? For example, does the opening briefly state the problem and establish its importance?

☐ yes ☐ no   Comments:_____

3. Does the writer explain the problem in a second paragraph using reasons, facts, or examples?

☐ yes ☐ no   Comments:_____

4. Is each of the solutions in a separate paragraph?

☐ yes ☐ no   Comments:_____

5. Are the solutions reasonable?

☐ yes ☐ no   Comments:_____

6. Are the solutions possible? In other words, can they be done?

☐ yes ☐ no   Comments:_____

6. Does the writer stick to the topic?

☐ yes ☐ no   Comments:_____

7. Does the writer use transitional words to connect paragraphs and ideas within paragraphs?

☐ yes ☐ no   Comments:_____

8. Does the writer use interesting words and phrases?

☐ yes ☐ no   Comments:_____

9. Does the writer use different types of sentences to make the essay interesting?

☐ yes   ☐ no   Comments:_____

10. Does the essay have a strong closing? For example, does it make another statement about the importance of the problem and the need to solve it?

☐ yes   ☐ no   Comments:_____

Decide what changes would improve your essay, and make these changes on your paper. Remember that these sorts of improvements can make a difference in your test score.

For extra practice, make a final copy of your revised essay. This time, proofread it carefully and make sure that the grammar, punctuation, and spelling are all correct.

4. THINKING ABOUT PROBLEMS AND SOLUTIONS

What problems may I be asked to solve on the EWT?

You won't know ahead of time, of course, but you can make a pretty good guess that the problems will be ones you are directly involved in. The problem could be a school-based one—like fighting. It could be a community problem—like drugs. It could be one that families face—like loss of a job. Or it could be problems that affect everyone—like pollution.

You prepared for this essay by thinking about your own problems. Now, work with your classmates to prepare another survey of current problems in—

- Your school

- Your community

- Your family

- The world

Identifying problems is just the first step. Work with partners in your class to think about possible solutions. Spend time each week discussing current problems and possible solutions.

Part 2 of the Writing Test

6. The Multiple-Choice Test

What is the second part of the Early Warning Test?

The second part of the EWT Writing test is a test of your ability to revise and edit what someone else has written.

This part of the EWT consists of several sample passages that need revision. The passages are similar to ones you and your classmates might write. They may include—

- A letter to a friend or a relative
- A letter to a newspaper editor or an advice columnist
- A letter of complaint
- An opinion essay on a movie, a video, or a music album
- A science or social studies essay written as a class assignment
- A book or story report

Each passage also includes writing mistakes that students your age often make.

After each passage there are 8 multiple-choice questions. Each question refers to some part of the passage and asks you what—if anything—needs editing or revising there. Your job is to pick the answer choice that has the correct revision or the best revision.

What skills do I need in order to do well in this test?

You will need to know how to do the following:

- Recognize and correct errors in capitalization, punctuation, and spelling
- Correct nonstandard usage
- Add something to a sentence to make it logical
- Combine ideas into one sentence
- Use transition words to show how ideas are connected
- Organize ideas by selecting main ideas and supporting details and by rearranging or adding sentences

This chapter will show you how to do each of these.

How can I prepare for this part of the test?

If you completed the first unit of this book, you have already started. In the first unit, you practiced revising the work of other writers. Often it is easier to see the mistakes other people make than it is to spot your own errors.

This second unit of **The EWT Coach** gives you specific, on-target help with the second part of the EWT.

- Part I of this unit contains 6 *Sample Test Passages*. Each passage is followed by several multiple choice questions, just like the ones you will work with on the real test.

  A special section called *Answers, Strategies, and Tips* follows the questions. This section discusses each question individually. The discussion gives correct answers, explains why the wrong answers are wrong, and gives strategies and tips for dealing with that particular kind of question. Each discussion also refers you to a section in the "Skills and Practice Handbook" at the end of this book, where you will find a short description of the skill or rule that the question is testing.

- Part II of this unit of the book is a *Skills and Practice Handbook* that contains all the skills and rules that are tested on the EWT. If you got an answer wrong, or if you got the correct answer but are not sure why it is correct, go to the indicated part of the "Skills and Practice." To get a general idea of all skills, you will need to sharpen, read and practice the entire section.

- Part II of this unit consists of a final set of 6 *Practice Tests*. When you feel ready, take the final set of Practice Tests.

Your teacher will also suggest that you make a note of any spelling words or rules of grammar, usage, and punctuation that you have trouble with. You will want to pay special attention to them when you revise your own work or when you edit the work of someone else.

7. Sample Test Passages with Answers, Strategies, and Tips

PASSAGE A

Janell has written this letter to the manufacturer of a tape player she bought recently. Her letter explains why she is returning the tape player. She has asked you to look over the letter and help her improve it before she sends it.

Read the letter carefully and help Janell improve her organization, revise her sentence structure, and correct her mechanics. Feel free to write in the text as you read, revise, and edit the letter.

1 April 7, 1992

2 Dear President of the Personal Cassette Player Company:

3 I bought this tape player last week. I'm sending it back to

4 you because it doesnt work very well.

5 There are two problems. The first one is that it sounds funny

6 when I walk fast or jog, it's fine when I stand still, but the

7 music sounds blurry when I exercise. I bought this tape player to

8 use when I exercise. I don't want it anymor if it usually works

9 only when I stand still.

10 The second problem is that it won't stay hooked on my belt.

11 The headphones get unplugged, and the tape player falls off.

12 It might get broke or lost falling off that way. I know I

13 could put it in my pocket. I don't always have a pocket in my

14 pants or shirt. Besides, I shouldn't have to wear special clothes

15 to use my tape player.

16 Anyway, this is what I'd like to do. If you agree I would

17 like to have my money back.

18 Sincerely yours,

Janell Rivera

19 Janell Rivera

86

1. How should Janell revise the first sentence in line 3 ("*I . . . week.*") to make its meaning clearer?

   A. I bought this stupid tape player from you last week.
   B. Last week I bought one of the tape players that you advertised in the paper.
   C. Last week I bought the Personal Tape Player, Model 0-5, that you advertised in the <u>Herald-Beacon</u>.
   D. I bought a Personal Tape Player from you last week because it looked so great in your advertisement.

2. What revision, if any, should Janell make at the end of the sentence in lines 3-4 ("*I'm . . . well.*")?

   A. Change *doesnt* to **doesn't**.
   B. Change *well* to **good**.
   C. Change *doesnt* to **don't**.
   D. Make no change.

3. Which editing change should Janell make to correct the run-on in the sentence in lines 5-7 ("*The . . . exercise.*")?

   A. Add a period after *funny* and start a new sentence with **When**.
   B. Change the **comma** after *jog* to a **period** and start a new sentence with **It's**.
   C. Change the **comma** after *still* to a **period** and start a new sentence with **But**.
   D. Add a period after *blurry* and start a new sentence with **When**.

4. Which editing change should Janell make in line 8?

   A. Change *anymor* to **any more**.
   B. Change *usually* to **usualy**.
   C. Change *anymor* to **anymore**.
   D. Change *usually* to **usally**.

5. How should Janell revise the sentence in line 12 ("*It . . . way.*")?

   A. Change *might get* to **might of got**.
   B. Change *might get* to **might have gotten**.
   C. Change *broke* to **broked**.
   D. Change *broke* to **broken**.

6. What is the best way for Janell to combine the two sentences in lines 12-14 ("*I know . . . shirt.*")?

   A. I know I could put it in my pocket since I don't always have a pocket in my pants or shirt.
   B. I know I could put it in my pocket, but I don't always have a pocket in my pants or shirt.
   C. I know I could put it in my pocket, and I don't always have a pocket in my pants or shirt.
   D. I know I could put it in my pocket if I don't always have a pocket in my pants or shirt.

7. Which sentence would be <u>best</u> to omit from this letter?

   A. Line 5 ("*There . . . problems.*")
   B. Lines 7-8 ("*I bought . . . exercise.*")
   C. Lines 14-15 ("*Besides . . . player.*")
   D. Line 16 ("*Anyway . . . do.*")

8. What editing change, if any, should Janell make in the sentence in lines 16-17 ("*If . . . back.*")?

   A. Add a **comma** between *agree* and *I*.
   B. Add a **comma** between *would* and *like*.
   C. Add a **comma** between *like* and *to*.
   D. Make no change.

PASSAGE A — ANSWERS, STRATEGIES, AND TIPS

QUESTION 1: *See "Skills & Practice," page 140.*

Revising a sentence "to make its meaning clearer" usually means adding information to the sentence. All four answer choices have something added to them.

- **Choice C** is the correct answer because it supplies the greatest amount of specific information.
- Choices B and D each add some of this information, but not all of it.
- Choice A doesn't add real information—just the word "stupid," which is not appropriate when you are writing this kind of letter.

QUESTION 2: *See "Skills & Practice," page 132.*

The words "editing change" or "revision" often mean a change in punctuation, capitalization, spelling, or usage. Ask yourself, "Has the writer selected the correct word? Is the word written correctly?"

- **Choice A** is the correct answer because the contraction ***doesn't*** needs an apostrophe between the ***n*** and the ***t***.
- Choice B would change the adverb ***well***, which is correct here, to the adjective ***good***, which is not correct.
- Choice C is not standard written English.

QUESTION 3: *See "Skills & Practice," pages 136-37.*

The question tells you that Janell needs to correct a run-on.

- **Choice B** is the correct answer because you need either to insert a period or to put in a comma plus a word like ***and*** or ***but*** between the two parts of a run-on sentence like this.
- The other three choices would also start new sentences, but they would leave this error—the comma between ***jog*** and ***it's***—unchanged.
- Choice D is wrong for an additional reason: the new sentence beginning with ***When*** is really a fragment.

QUESTION 4:

This question asks about the spelling of two words and gives you two choices for each one.

- **Choice C** is correct because ***anymore*** should be written as one word when it is an adverb meaning "any longer."
- Choice A is incorrect because the form ***any more*** should be used to modify a noun. It answers the question "How much?" ("I don't want any more ice cream.")
- Choices B and D are both incorrect spellings of ***usually***.

QUESTION 5: *See "Skills & Practice," page 135.*
All four choices ask about the same group of words—*might get broke*, so you
know that this is a question about verb usage.

- **Choice D** is correct because the past participle of *break* is *broken*
  (*break, broke, broken*).
- Choices A-C fail to make this correction.
  In addition, Choice A contains another error in verb usage (*might of got*
  for *might have got* (or *might have gotten*).
- Choice B is an unnecessary change (though the verb forms in it are
  correct).
- Choice C makes a change to an incorrect verb form (the past participle of
  break is not *broked.*)

QUESTION 6: *See "Skills & Practice," page 141.*
When you are asked for the "best way" to combine two or more sentences, look
for the answer that keeps the writer's meaning unchanged. In this case, all four
choices are alike except for the word that connects the two sentences.

- **Choice B** is the correct answer because it expresses contrast: I could put
  it in my pocket; <u>however</u>, I don't always have a pocket.
- Choice A is incorrect because *since* has the meaning of "because." Using
  this word changes the author's meaning.
- In Choice C, *and* means "also"; in Choice D, *if* means "on the condition
  that." Both choices change the author's meaning.

QUESTION 7: *See "Skills & Practice," page 142.*
When you are asked what should be omitted, look for a sentence that does not
stick to the main idea or that is repetitive.

- **Choice D** is the correct answer in this case because the first sentence in
  line 17 is unnecessary. It doesn't say anything new.
- In choices A-C, the sentences contain important information or ideas
  that are not found in other sentences. They should not be dropped.

QUESTION 8: *See "Skills & Practice," page 130.*
Notice that the answer choices all ask about adding a comma to the sentence.

- **Choice A** is correct because an introductory group of words like *If you
  agree* is usually followed by a comma.
- Choices B and C add commas in places where they are not needed.
- Choice D is wrong because a change is needed—the change suggested in
  Choice A.

Hector wrote the following book report for his English class. He asked you to look it over for him and help him improve it before he turns it in.

Read the report carefully and help him improve his organization, revise his sentence structure, and correct his mechanics. Feel free to write in the text as you read, revise, and edit the report.

1	<u>Whistle while You Work</u>
2	A Book Report by Hector Jordan
3	In the book <u>Whistle while You Work</u>, by Eugene Sears, two boys
4	start a business of their own. These two guys are friends, and they
5	are only fourteen years old. They spend a lot of time looking for
6	summer jobs. There's one problem. All the jobs have been taken by
7	kids who are older.
8	Then the two friends decide something. By the way, their names
9	are Dean and J.J. They decide to get a lot of small jobs instead of
10	one big job. They go all around the neighborhood and ask everybody
11	to give them just one thing to do. For example, J.J. says to the
12	guy who owns the pizza place, "Let Dean and I wash your delivery
13	truck for you once a week."
14	In the end Dean and J.J. are right. Their plan works because
15	nobody ever has enough time to do everything. Nearly everybody
16	has one job that there isn't time for. I'd like to try this way
17	of making money myself. They sweep the floors in one place. In
18	another place they clean the refrigerator. Soon people are calling
19	them up and asking them to do things.
20	I liked this book. It might not be completely realistic but
21	it was a lot of fun to read. It also gave me some good ideas for
22	ways to make money.

9. What editing change, if any, should Hector make to the title of the book in lines 1 and 3?

   A. "Whistle while You Work"
   B. Whistle while you Work
   C. Whistle While You Work
   D. Make no change

10. What transition should Hector add to the beginning of the sentence in line 6 ("There's...problem.")?

    A. However,
    B. Finally,
    C. In addition,
    D. Well,

11. What is the best way for Hector to combine the three sentences in lines 8-10 ("Then...job.") into one sentence?

    A. The two friends are named Dean and J.J., and they decide to get a lot of small jobs instead of one big job.
    B. Dean and J.J. are the two friends who decide to get a lot of small jobs instead of one big job.
    C. Getting a lot of small jobs instead of one big job is what Dean and J.J. decide to do.
    D. The two friends, Dean and J.J., decide to get a lot of small jobs instead of one big job.

12. What editing change, if any, is needed in line 10?

    A. Change *all around* to **all round**.
    B. Change *neighborhood* to **nieghborhood**.
    C. Change *everybody* to **every body**.
    D. Make no change.

13. What editing change is needed in line 12?

    A. Remove the **comma** after *place*.
    B. Change *Let* to **let**.
    C. Change *I* to **me**.
    D. Change *your* to **you're**.

14. What editing change, if any, should Hector make in line 14 of his book report?

    A. Add a **comma** between *end* and *Dean*.
    B. Change *Their* to **There**.
    C. Change *Their* to **Their'**.
    D. Make no change.

15. All of the following sentences support the main idea of the third paragraph (lines 14-19) EXCEPT

    A. *Nearly everybody has one job that there isn't time for.*
    B. *I'd like to try this way of making money myself.*
    C. *They sweep the floors in one place.*
    D. *Soon people are calling them up and asking them to do things.*

16. What editing change, if any, should Hector make in the sentence in lines 20-21 ("It...read.")?

    A. Change *completely* to **completly**.
    B. Add a **comma** after *realistic*.
    C. Change *a lot* to **alot**.
    D. Make no change.

PASSAGE B — ANSWERS, STRATEGIES, AND TIPS

QUESTION 9: *See "Skills & Practice," page 124.*

An editing change in a title will usually involve capitalization and underlining or quotation marks. Since this is the title of a book, it has to be underlined.

- **Choice C** is correct because it is underlined, and all the necessary words begin with capital letters.
- Choice A is not underlined, and in choices B and D there are words that need to begin with a capital letter.

QUESTION 10: *See "Skills & Practice," page 141.*

A transition at the beginning of a sentence should connect this sentence in a logical way to the one before it.

- **Choice A** is correct because *However* makes the most sense. It indicates a contrast (they are looking for jobs, <u>but</u> there's a problem).
- Choices B-D do not express logical connections for these sentences.

QUESTION 11: *See "Skills & Practice," page 141.*

Remember that when you combine sentences, the result needs to make sense, to sound smooth, and to keep the writer's original meaning.

- **Choice D** is correct because it does all these things.
- Choice A makes the boys' names the most important part of the sentence.
- Choice B emphasizes *are the two friends*.
- Choice C leaves out the fact that Dean and J.J. are friends, and it uses an awkward sentence construction.

QUESTION 12:

Notice that all the choices in this question are about how words are written or spelled.

- **Choice D** is correct because *everybody* is written as one word when it means "everyone." Therefore, no change should be made in this sentence.
- Choices A-C are incorrect ways of writing or spelling these words.

QUESTION 13: *See "Skills & Practice," page 136.*

Notice that the choices in this question have to do with punctuation, capitalization, and word choice.

- **Choice C** is correct because after the verb *let*, you need the object form of the pronoun—*me*.
- Choices A and B are not correct because you need a comma after the words that introduce a quotation, and the first word of the quotation should begin with a capital letter.
- Choice D is not correct because *your* is a possessive pronoun in this sentence, not a contraction of a pronoun and a verb.

QUESTION 14: *See "Skills & Practice," page 129.*

- **Choice A** is correct because an introductory group of words like this one is set off by a comma.
- Choices B and C are incorrect because *Their* is a possessive pronoun and is not written with an apostrophe.

QUESTION 15: *See "Skills & Practice," page 142.*

In order to answer this question, you need to know what the main idea of the third paragraph is.

- **Choice B** is correct because this sentence digresses; it does not stay on the topic of how Dean and J.J. earn money.
- All the other answer choices support the main idea—how Dean and J.J. make money.

QUESTION 16: *See "Skills & Practice," page 127.*

- **Choice B** is correct because when you use <u>but</u> to join two sentences, you need to add a comma before <u>but</u>.
- Choices A and C are incorrect spellings.
- Choice D is wrong because you need to make the change in B.

Kim wrote this report for her social studies class. She would like you to read it and help her improve it before she turns it in.

Read the report carefully and help her improve her organization, revise her sentence structure, and correct her mechanics. Feel free to write in the text as you read, revise, and edit the report.

1   A Special Place in Newark

2   by Kim Johnson

3   The Newark Public Library is more than one hundred years old.

4   It opened in 1889 on West Park Street in Newark New Jersey. A

5   few years later, the city built a new building for the library

6   on Washington Street. This building was very large and granite

7   and marble. It opened in 1901, and the library is still in the

8   same place.

9   The most famous librarian was John Cotton Dana. He wanted the

10   library to be "a people's library" right from the start. Many of the

11   people living in Newark were immigrants. From other countries. The

12   library had books in lots of different languages. It also had books

13   about lots of different subjects. Mr. Dana gave reading lists to

14   everyone in Newark. He puts some of the library books in public

15   schools. As you can see, Mr. Dana did everything possible to get

16   people to read.

17   There were also art exhibits in the library. Mr. Dana did not

18   like modern art very much. However, he encouraged many modern artists.

19   He made the Newark Public Library an important center for art. It

20   was a place where people came to learn. It still is, and that's why

21   it's a special place to visit.

17. What editing change, if any, should Kim make in line 3 of her report?

    A. Change *Newark Public Library* to **Newark public library**.
    B. Change *Library* to **Libary**.
    C. Change *years* to **years'**.
    D. Make no change.

18. What editing change does Kim need to make in the sentence in line 4 of her report ("*It...Jersey.*")?

    A. Add a **comma** after *opened*.
    B. Add a **comma** after *West*.
    C. Change *Street* to **street**.
    D. Add a **comma** after *Newark*.

19. How should Kim revise the sentence in lines 6-7 ("*This...marble.*") to make its meaning clearer?

    A. This was a very large building and was also granite and marble.
    B. This building was made of very large granite and marble.
    C. This building was very large and made of granite and marble.
    D. This very large building made granite and marble.

20. What is the best way for Kim to revise lines 10 and 11 ("*Many...countries.*") in order to correct the fragment?

    A. From other countries, many of the people living in Newark were immigrants.
    B. Many of the people living in Newark were immigrants from other countries.
    C. Many of the people living in Newark were immigrants; from other countries.
    D. Many of the people from other countries living in Newark were immigrants.

21. What change should Kim make in line 14 of her report?

    A. Change *puts* to **did put**.
    B. Change *puts* to **put**.
    C. Change *puts* to **is putting**.
    D. Change *puts* to **putted**.

22. What editing change, if any, should Kim make in the last sentence of paragraph 2 ("*As...read.*")?

    A. Remove the **comma** after *see*.
    B. Add a **comma** after *Dana*.
    C. Add a **comma** after *possible*.
    D. Make no change.

23. What is the best way for Kim to combine the three sentences in lines 17-19 ("*Mr. . . art.*")?

    A. Encouraging modern artists even though he did not like modern art very much, Mr. Dana made Newark an important center for art.
    B. Making Newark an important center for art and encouraging modern artists, Mr. Dana did not like modern art very much.
    C. Encouraging modern artists, Newark became an important center for art even though Mr. Dana did not like modern art very much.
    D. Mr. Dana encouraged modern artists not liking modern art very much and made Newark an important art center.

24. Which sentence best states the main idea of Kim's report?

    A. The Newark Public Library is a very old building.
    B. People who like to read are also interested in art.
    C. The Newark Public Library has an interesting history.
    D. Old buildings can be very interesting to visit.

PASSAGE C — ANSWERS, STRATEGIES, AND TIPS

QUESTION 17: *See "Skills & Practice," pages 124-26.*
Notice that the answer choices ask you to make decisions about changes in capitalization, spelling, and punctuation. To answer this question, you need to look at the way line 3 is written.

- **Choice D** is correct because line 3 does not need to be changed in any way.
- Choice A is wrong because ***Newark Public Library*** is correctly written with a capital letter at the start of each word.
- Choice B is wrong because ***Library*** is spelled correctly.
- Choice C is wrong because ***years*** is not a possessive, so it is correct without an apostrophe.

QUESTION 18: *See "Skills & Practice," page 128.*
This sentence contains dates and names of places, so there are questions about punctuation and capitalization.

- **Choice D** is correct because you need a comma between the city and the state.
- Choices A and B are not correct because commas are not needed in either of these places.
- Choice C is incorrect because the word ***street*** is part of the address and needs to start with a capital letter.

QUESTION 19: *See "Skills & Practice," pages 139-40.*
To answer this question, you need to decide how the sentence should be reworded or what should be added to it to make the meaning clearer.

- **Choice C** is correct because the words ***made of*** make it clear that there are two parallel facts: The building was large; the building was made of marble and granite.
- The other answer choices change the meaning of the sentence rather than making it clearer.

QUESTION 20: *See "Skills & Practice," page 136.*
This question tells you that you need to correct a fragment. All the answer choices make the fragment ***From other countries*** part of the sentence. However—

- **Choice B** is correct because it does the best job of combining the sentence and the fragment that follows it.
- In Choices A and D, ***from other countries*** is placed too far from the word ***immigrants***, which it modifies.
- In Choice C, the semicolon between ***immigrants*** and ***from other countries*** is incorrect.

QUESTION 21: *See "Skills & Practice," page 135.*
Notice that all of the answer choices involve the form of the verb in this sentence. Since the rest of this paragraph is in the past tense, this sentence needs to be, too.

- **Choice B** is correct because the past tense form of ***put*** is **put**.
- In choices A and C the verb tenses are not consistent with the rest of the paragraph.
- Choice D has an incorrect verb form.

QUESTION 22: *See "Skills & Practice," page 130.*
Notice that all the choices ask about adding or removing commas.

- You need to read the sentence to see that **Choice D** is correct. You don't need to make any changes in this sentence.
- Choice A is incorrect because the introductory words ***As you can see*** need to be followed by a comma.
- Choices B and C add commas where they are not needed.

QUESTION 23: *See "Skills & Practice," page 141.*
Remember that when sentences are combined, they have to make sense and sound smooth.

- **Choice A** is correct because it keeps the original meaning: Mr. Dana encouraged modern artists even though he did not like modern art; by encouraging modern artists, he made Newark an important center for art.
- In the other answer choices, one or more parts of the combined sentences are placed so that this meaning is garbled or unclear.

QUESTION 24: *See "Skills & Practice," page 142.*
In order to answer this question, you need to think about the whole report, not just one paragraph. Ask yourself, what do all the paragraphs in this report have in common?

- Each paragraph tells something interesting about the history of the Newark Public Library, so **Choice C** is the correct answer.
- Choice A is only one detail in this report.
- Choices B and D are conclusions you might be able to draw from this report, but none of these choices states the main idea of the <u>whole</u> report.

PASSAGE D

Charles has broken his leg and will be out of school for two weeks. The whole class is writing him letters to cheer him up. Your teacher has asked you to work with a partner to revise and edit your letters before you send them.

Gus is your partner. Read his letter carefully and help him improve his organization, revise his sentence structure, and correct his mechanics. Feel free to write in the text as you revise and edit.

1   May 23, 1993

2   Dear Charles,

3   You must have really been surprised when you fell out of that

4   tree in the park and busted your leg. I guess it hurt a lot. What

5   did it feel like when the doctor had to push the bones back together?

6   Did it make a crunching sound?

7   Not too much is happening. Ms. Coleman was out one day we had

8   a substitute named Mr. Jarvis. I guess he didn't want to do any

9   of the stuff Ms. Coleman left for him. Anyway, we played all kinds

10   of games instead, like Spelling Bee and Geography Trivia. The winner

11   of each game got a prize. I won this weird pencil that looks all

12   twisted.

13   Most of the time school is just ordinary, like it usually is.

14   We read some more stories in the literature book. We wrote book

15   reports. We did another chapter in the math book. We started

16   our science project. In fact, it's pretty boring without you

17   around, except the most funniest thing happened in gym class.

18   We had a fire drill. Then when we were coming in, the

19   alarm went off again, and nobody knew which way to go.

20   See how much fun you're missing Charles? Get well soon.

21   Your pal,

                                                          Gus Henkel

22   Gus Henkel

98

25. Which of the following would be the best first sentence for Gus's letter?

A. The whole class was sorry to hear about your accident.

B. We were wondering why you weren't in school this week.

C. How high was the tree that you climbed in Brooks Park?

D. Are you lucky to have an excuse to stay home and watch TV!

26. What editing change, if any, should Gus make in line 4 of his letter?

A. Change *busted* to **broken**.
B. Change *busted* to **bust**.
C. Change *busted* to **broke**.
D. Make no change.

27. What is the best way for Gus to revise the first sentence in paragraph 2 ("*Not...happening.*") to make it more logical?

A. As usual, not too much is happening.

B. Not too much is happening here in school.

C. Not too much is happening at home right now.

D. Even though you're out, not too much is happening.

28. What is the best way for Gus to revise the sentence in lines 7-8 ("*Ms....Jarvis.*")?

A. Ms. Coleman was out one day, we had a substitute named Mr. Jarvis.

B. Ms. Coleman was out one day and we had a substitute named Mr. Jarvis.

C. Ms. Coleman was out one day that we had a substitute named Mr. Jarvis.

D. Ms. Coleman was out one day; we had a substitute named Mr. Jarvis.

29. Which sentence should Gus add at the begining of paragraph 3 (line 7) to make a smoother transition?

A. Anyway, you know how school is.
B. The pencil doesn't write very well.
C. Don't worry that you missed a lot of fun, though.
D. Ms. Coleman was back the next day.

30. What is the best way for Gus to combine the four sentences in lines 14-16 ("We...project.")?

A. We read some more stories in the literature book, wrote book reports, another chapter in the math book, and our science project.

B. We read some more stories in the literature book, wrote book reports, did another chapter in the math book, and started our science project.

C. We read some more stories in the literature book, writing book reports, doing another chapter in the math book, and starting our science project.

D. We read some more stories in the literature book, and wrote book reports, and did another chapter in the math book, and started our science project.

31. What editing change should Gus make in line 17 of his letter?

A. Change *most funniest* to **funnier**.
B. Change *most funniest* to **funiest**.
C. Change *most funniest* to **most funnyest**.
D. Change *most funniest* to **funniest**.

32. What editing change should Gus make in line 20 of his letter?

A. Add a **comma** after *See*.
B. Add a **comma** after *fun*.
C. Add a **comma** after *missing*.
D. Add a **comma** after *well*.

PASSAGE D — ANSWERS, STRATEGIES, AND TIPS

QUESTION 25: *See "Skills & Practice," page 142.*
The important words in this question are "best first sentence." The first sentence of the letter should introduce the whole letter and should make sense as the opening of the first paragraph.

- **Choice A** is the correct answer because it explains why Gus is writing this letter, and it expresses concern for Charles.
- Choices B and C don't mention his accident or injury.
- Choice D doesn't show any concern for how Charles is feeling.

QUESTION 26: *See "Skills & Practice," page 135.*
Notice that the answer choices all involve the past tense form of the verb in this sentence.

- **Choice C** is correct because **broke** is the correct past tense form of **break**.
- Choice A, **broken**, is the form used after **have** or **had**. It is the past participle of **break**, not the past tense.
- Choices B and D are not standard written English.

QUESTION 27: *See "Skills & Practice," page 140.*
When you are asked to make a sentence more logical, you usually need to add or change something.

- **Choice B** is the correct answer because it tells <u>where</u> "not too much is happening."
- Choice A is too general.
- Choice C is incorrect (**at home**).
- Choice D is not logical.

QUESTION 28: *See "Skills & Practice," pages 136-37.*
Notice that all the answer choices consist of two sentences that have been joined in some way. This question is asking you the best way to correct a run-on.

- **Choice D** is the correct answer because it uses a semicolon to join the two sentences.
- Choice A has only a comma, without a word like <u>and</u>.
- Choice B has only <u>and</u> without a comma.
- In Choice C, **that** does not connect the two sentences as well as **and** or a semicolon.

QUESTION 29: *See "Skills & Practice," page 142.*
To answer this question, find the main idea in paragraph 2.

- Now you can see that **Choice C** is the correct answer because it refers to the main idea of paragraph 2—the fun that the class has been having—and connects it to the main idea of paragraph 3—that most of the time school is ordinary.
- Choice A is too general.
- Choice B refers only to the last sentence in paragraph 2.
- Choice D refers to a fact that is implied but not stated in paragraph 3.

QUESTION 30: *See "Skills & Practice," page 138.*
When you combine sentences to make a list, the items in the list must be parallel.

- **Choice B** is correct because the four items in the list are all parallel: they all have the same structure, with verbs in the same form (***read, wrote, did, started***).
- In Choices A and C, the items are not parallel.
- Choice D repeats **and** unnecessarily.

QUESTION 31: *See "Skills & Practice," page 137.*
All four answer choices are about the form of the adjective *funny*.

- **Choice D** is the correct answer because it adds *-est* to the word **funny** to compare more than two things.
- Choice A adds *-er*, which should be used just for comparing two things.
- Choice B misspells **funniest**.
- Choice C adds both **most** and **-est** instead of just one; it also misspells **funniest**.

QUESTION 32: *See "Skills & Practice," page 129.*

- **Choice C** is the correct answer because you need a comma before the name of a person to whom you are speaking directly.
- The commas in Choices A, B, and D are all unnecessary.

LaVerne's class is writing letters to the advice columnist in the local newspaper. Before you send the letters, you are reading what each other has written and making suggestions for revision.

Read LaVerne's letter carefully and help her improve her organization, revise her sentence structure, and correct her mechanics. Feel free to write in the text as you read, revise, and edit the letter.

1   April 23, 1992

2   Dear Ms. Lincoln:

3   In your "Tell Me" column this week you asked what advice

4   we eighth-graders would give to kids who are going to be in

5   eighth grade next year? This is what I would tell a new eighth-

6   grader.

7   If you want to be a success in eighth grade, you need to work

8   hard in seventh grade. You need to do good in all your classes,

9   especially reading and math, so that the work in eighth grade

10   won't be too hard for you. Teachers don't be mean on purpose,

11   but they won't be easy on you either. It's good to be able to

12   write a good essay too. You will get better grades if you know

13   how to write an essay. Lots of teachers ask you to write essays.

14   Just because you're graduating you can't stop working.

15   You still have to study and get the assignments done. I would

16   also tell students to keep working hard in eighth grade. They

17   give you all kinds of new stuff in eighth grade that you need

18   for high school.

19   With my advice, your readers should have a great year in

20   eighth grade.

                                   Sincerely,

                                   LaVerne Towson

22   LaVerne Towson

33. What editing change, if any, should LaVerne make in line 3 of her letter?

   A. Insert a **comma** after the word *Me*.
   B. Insert a **comma** after the word *week*.
   C. Insert a **comma** after the word *asked*.
   D. Make no change.

34. What editing change, if any, should LaVerne make in line 4 of her letter?

   A. Change *we* to **us**.
   B. Change *eighth-graders* to **eigth-graders**.
   C. Change *give* to **have gave**.
   D. Make no change.

35. What editing change, if any, should LaVerne make in line 5 of her letter?

   A. Change the **question mark** after *year* to a **period**.
   B. Change the **question mark** after *year* to a **colon**.
   C. Change the **question mark** after *year* to a **comma** and change *This* to **this**.
   D. Make no change.

36. How should LaVerne revise the sentence in lines 8-10 of her letter ("*You...you.*")?

   A. Change *good* to **well**.
   B. Change *your* to **your'**.
   C. Change *especially* to **especialy**.
   D. Change *too* to **to**.

37. How would you revise the sentence in lines 10-11 ("*Teachers...either.*") to help LaVerne use standard written English?

   A. Teachers won't be mean on purpose, but they won't be easy on you neither.
   B. Teachers won't be mean on purpose, but they won't be easy on you either.
   C. Teachers don't be mean on purpose, but they don't be easy on you either.
   D. Teachers don't be mean on purpose, but they don't be easy on you neither.

38. What is the best way for LaVerne to combine the three sentences in lines 11-13 ("*It's...essays.*")

   A. Knowing how to write a good essay, your grades will be better because lots of teachers ask you to write essays.
   B. Lots of teachers will ask you to write essays, so knowing how to write a good essay, your grades will be better.
   C. In addition, since lots of teachers ask you to write essays, you will get better grades if you can write a good essay.
   D. You will get better grades in addition, with lots of teachers asking you to write essays, if you can write a good essay.

39. Which change in organization would best improve the <u>third</u> paragraph of LaVerne's letter?

   A. Move the first sentence to the end of the paragraph.
   B. Move the second sentence to the beginning of the paragraph.
   C. Place the second sentence between the third and fourth sentences.
   D. Move the third sentence to the beginning of the paragraph.

40. How should LaVerne revise the last sentence in paragraph 3 (lines 16-18) to make it clearer?

   A. In eighth grade you learn important stuff that they teach you for high school.
   B. Your teachers give you new supplies in eighth grade to prepare you for high school.
   C. You learn all kinds of new things in eighth grade that you need for high school.
   D. Eighth grade is important for learning stuff they think you need for high school.

PASSAGE E — ANSWERS, STRATEGIES, AND TIPS

QUESTION 33: *See "Skills & Practice," page 129.*
Since the answer choices all involve inserting commas, look first at the passage to see whether any commas are needed in line 3.

- This sentence begins with a long introductory group of words, so **Choice B** is the correct answer. A comma is needed after an introductory group of words like this one.
- Choices A and C would add commas where they are not needed.

QUESTION 34: *See "Skills & Practice," page 135.*
The answer choices involve usage and spelling, so you need to see whether there are any usage or spelling errors in line 4.

- **Choice D** is correct because there are no errors.
- Choice A would make the object form of the pronoun—*us*—the subject.
- Choice B is an incorrect spelling, and
- Choice C uses an incorrect form of the verb *give*.

QUESTION 35: *See "Skills & Practice," page 127.*
Notice that all these answer choices involve the punctuation at the end of the sentence.

- The correct answer is **Choice A** because this sentence is a statement, not a question.
- Choices B and C are incorrect because they suggest that this sentence might be a fragment or needs to be combined with the next sentence for some other reason.

QUESTION 36: *See "Skills & Practice," page 138.*
Again, the answer choices involve usage and spelling.

- **Choice A** is correct because following the verb *do* in this sentence, you need an adverb (*well*), not an adjective.
- Choice B would add an apostrophe to a possessive pronoun that is written without an apostrophe.
- Choice C is an incorrect spelling.
- Choice D is an incorrect word choice for this sentence.

QUESTION 37: *See "Skills & Practice," page 139.*
The key words in this question are "standard written English." Look at where the answer choices are alike and where they are different. You can see that the choices involve **won't be** and **don't be** and **either** and **neither**.

- **Choice B** is the correct answer because **won't be** is the standard written English form for both parts of this sentence. In addition, **either**, rather than **neither**, is standard written English when there is already a negative expressed in the sentence.
- Choices A, C, and D all contain expressions that are not standard written English.

QUESTION 38: *See "Skills & Practice," page 141.*
To answer this question, think about whether each choice makes sense.

- The correct answer is **Choice B** because the pieces of the sentence have been arranged in an order that makes sense and because the words **In addition**, **since**, and **if** help make the meaning clear.
- In answer choices A, C, and D, the parts of the sentence have not been arranged as logically.

QUESTION 39: *See "Skills & Practice," page 142.*
When you see the words "change in organization," you are being asked about moving a sentence from one place to another. To answer the question, think about how the sentences in paragraph 3 are connected.

- The correct answer is **Choice D** because this makes the best opening sentence for the paragraph.
- The sentences in choices A-C make more sense where they are.

QUESTION 40: *See "Skills & Practice," page 140.*
Remember that when you are asked to revise to make something clearer, words will be added or changed to provide more details.

- **Choice C** is the correct answer because it gets rid of the vague words **they** and **stuff** and makes the meaning of the sentence clearer.
- Answer choices A and D are less clear.
- Answer choice B is more specific but changes the meaning of the sentence.

Omar wrote the following review of a new TV show for his English class. He asked you to look it over for him and help him improve it before he turns it in.

Read the review carefully and help him improve his organization, revise his sentence structure, and correct his mechanics. Feel free to write in the text as you read, revise, and edit the review.

1	The New Duke and Dolly Show is on TV on Wednesday night at
2	7:30. It's supposed to be like last year's show, only better. In
3	fact, the song at the beginning says, "The new improved Duke and
4	Dolly." It is a new song and the drawings for the titles are new, too.
5	I can't see too much that's new in this show. The improvements are
6	very small. They include a different voice for Dolly. There's also
7	a new character named Tooner. And they've drawn a hat on Duke's
8	head. I agree that all these things help make the show a little
9	better. It's definitely more lively now. Basically, though,
10	you're still watching the same old cartoon about two funny-looking
11	animals that sing and dance.
12	Of course, it was pretty good. It was always funny, and it
13	had great music. Kids loved it, and even some parents watched
14	it every week. My favorite episode was the one about Thanksgiving
15	dinner. The new show is like the old show in some important
16	ways. Duke and Dolly have the same kinds of problems that
17	kids do, like getting into trouble in school or at home.
18	My conclusion is that if you liked the old show, you will
19	like the new one. They aren't very different. I'm not sure
20	why the TV people thought they needed to improve the show.
21	Anyway, the changes aren't too big, and the show is still
22	good.

41. What editing change, if any, should Omar make in line 1 of his review?

   A. Change ***The New Duke and Dolly Show*** to **The New Duke And Dolly Show**.

   B. Change ***The New Duke and Dolly Show*** to **The New Duke and Dolly show**.

   C. Change ***The New Duke and Dolly Show*** to **The new Duke and Dolly show**.

   D. Make no change.

42. What editing change does Omar need to make in the sentence in lines 2-4 ("*In...Dolly.*") of his review?

   A. Take out the **comma** after the word *fact*.
   B. Insert a **comma** after the word *song*.
   C. Take out the **comma** after the word *says*.
   D. Insert a **comma** after the word *new*.

43. Which transition is needed at the beginning of paragraph 2?

   A. Because of that,
   B. In addition to that,
   C. However,
   D. Instead of that,

44. What is the best way to combine the four sentences in lines 5-8 ("*The...head.*")?

   A. The improvements, including a different voice for Dolly, a new character named Tooner, and a hat drawn on Duke's head, are very small.

   B. The improvements are very small: a different voice for Dolly, a new character named Tooner, and a hat drawn on Duke's head.

   C. Including a different voice for Dolly, a new character named Tooner, and a hat drawn on Duke's head, the improvements are very small.

   D. Including very small improvements are: a different voice for Dolly, a new character named Tooner, and a hat drawn on Duke's head.

45. Which editing change, if any, does Omar need to make in line 9 of his review?

   A. Change *It's* to **Its**.
   B. Change *more lively* to **more livelier**.
   C. Change *Basically* to **Basicly**.
   D. Make no change.

46. How should Omar revise the first sentence of paragraph 3 (line 12) to make it more logical?

   A. Of course, the old show was pretty good.
   B. Of course, the old show was pretty awful.
   C. As a result, the old show was pretty good.
   D. As a result, the old show was pretty awful.

47. All of the following sentences support the focus of the third paragraph (lines 12-17) EXCEPT

   A. *It was always funny, and it had great music.*

   B. *Kids loved it, and even some parents watched it every week.*

   C. *My favorite episode was the one about Thanksgiving dinner.*

   D. *The new show is like the old show in some important ways.*

48. Which sentence best states the controlling idea of Omar's review?

   A. The New Duke and Dolly Show is not very good because very few improvements have been made in it.

   B. The New Duke and Dolly Show is as good as the old one because it has not been changed too much.

   C. The New Duke and Dolly Show is much better than the old because some big improvements have been made.

   D. The New Duke and Dolly Show, like the old one, is not very interesting to either kids or their parents.

PASSAGE F — ANSWERS, STRATEGIES, AND TIPS

QUESTION 41: *See "Skills & Practice," page 124.*
As you can see from the answer choices, this question is about which words should be capitalized in a title.

- The answer is **Choice D** because the title is correct as it is written.
- Choice A capitalizes a word that should not begin with a capital.
- Choices B and C contain words that should begin with a capital letter but don't.

QUESTION 42: *See "Skills & Practice," page 128.*
The answer choices all involve inserting or taking out commas.

- The correct answer is **Choice D** because a comma is needed between two adjectives that both modify the same noun if the word "and" could be inserted between them.
- Choices A and C would take out commas that are required.
- Choice B would insert a comma where it is not needed.

QUESTION 43: *See "Skills & Practice," page 141.*
Remember that a transition makes a logical connection.

- The correct answer is **Choice C** because it expresses most accurately the way paragraph 1 is related to the first sentence of paragraph 2.
- Choices A, B, and D are not correct because they express other sorts of relationships.

QUESTION 44: *See "Skills & Practice," page 141.*
When you are asked to combine four sentences, one of the best ways is to write a sentence that contains a series of items.

- **Choice B** is correct because the part of the sentence that introduces the series is clear and logical.
- In answer choices A, C, and D, the part of the sentence that introduces the series doesn't always make sense.

QUESTION 45: *See "Skills & Practice," pages 132, 137.*
You need to decide first whether there are any errors in punctuation, spelling, or word choice.

- The correct answer is **Choice D** because line 9 is correct as written.
- Choice A would remove an apostrophe from a contraction where it is needed.
- In Choice B, you don't need both *more* and *-er*.
- Choice C is not a correct spelling.

QUESTION 46: *See "Skills & Practice," page 140.*
To answer this question, you need to decide first which part of the sentence is too vague or doesn't make sense.

- The correct answer is **Choice A** because it makes the most logical transition from paragraph 2 to paragraph 3.
- The other answer choices do not provide logical transitions.

QUESTION 47: *See "Skills & Practice," page 142.*
The key word here is **EXCEPT**. This word usually indicates that you need to look for the sentence that does <u>not</u> support the main idea, the sentence that does not stick to the topic. First, you need to make sure that you know what the main idea of the paragraph is.

- **Choice C** is the correct answer because it does not support the focus, or main idea, of the paragraph.
- All the other answer choices support the focus, which is a comparison of the good points in the old show and the new show.

QUESTION 48: *See "Skills & Practice," page 142.*
This is also a question about main idea. This time you need to look for the main idea of the whole passage. The answer choices are statements of the main idea, not sentences from the passage.

- The correct answer is **Choice B** because it is the most accurate statement of the main idea.
- The other answer choices are not accurate statements of the main idea.

8. *Final Test*

PASSAGE G

Tia has written a report for social studies class on a new state law that requires everyone thirteen years or younger to wear a helmet. She feels very strongly about this issue and wants you to help her make it the best.

Read the report carefully and help Tia improve her organization, revise her sentence structure, and correct her mechanics. Feel free to write in the text as you read, revise, and edit the letter.

1   I think the new Jersey law about wearing helmets should

2   be made tougher. You have to wear a helmet until your

3   thirteen. But children aren't the only victims of accidents.

4   Last year my older brother was biking home from his

5   job. He is only fifteen. He had an accident. A car was coming

6   out of the parking lot, and he never saw it. So he crashed

7   into it and was thrown to the sidewalk. Banging his head. He

8   didn't wake up for three days.

9   He's all right. The hospital took good care of him, and he

10   even had a special tutor who helped him keep up with his

11   school work. He would have flunked his exams without this

12   help. I wish he had been wearing a helmet. But the new law

13   wouldn't have protected him. He was fifteen when the

14   accident happened. Remember, he is sixteen now.

15   I feel that everyone should be protected from serious

16   injury. The doctor told us that some people have constant

17   hedaches or can no longer read or work with numbers. We need

18   a law that will make everyone wear helmets. Working people

19   need their health just as much as children.

1. Which editing change, if any, should Tia make in the sentence in lines 1-2. (*I think . . . tougher.*)?

   A. Change *law* to **Law**.
   B. Change *new* to **New**.
   C. Add commas before *about* and after *helmets*.
   D. Make no change.

2. What revision, if any, should Tia make in lines 2-3 (*"You . . . thirteen."*)?

   A. Change *have* to **had**.
   B. Change *wear* to **wore**.
   C. Change *your* to **you're**.
   D. Make no change.

3. What is the best way to combine the ideas in lines 4-5 (*"Last year . . . accident."*) ?

   A. Last year my older brother had an accident because he was coming home from his job on a bike.
   B. Coming home from his job, my brother who is older than me and is fifteen had an accident on his bike.
   C. Last year, my fifteen year old brother had an accident biking home from his job.
   D. Since he was on his bike, my brother had an accident coming home from work.

4. What revision, if any, should Tia make in lines 6-8 (*"So . . . days."*) to get rid of the sentence fragment (*"Banging . . . head."*)?

   A. Banging his head, he was thrown to the sidewalk after crashing into the car.
   B. So he crashed into it and was thrown to the sidewalk, banging his head.
   C. Banging his head, he didn't wake up for three days.
   D. Make no change.

5. What transition word is needed at the beginning of line 9?

   A. Eventually,
   B. Now
   C. Soon
   D. After

6. Which sentence is not needed in the third paragraph?

   A. Lines 11-12 (*"He would have . . . help."*)?
   B. Line 12 (*"I wish . . . helmet."*)?
   C. Lines 12-13 (*"But the new law . . . him."*)?
   D. Line 14 (*"Remember, he . . . now."*) ?

7. What editing change, if any, should Tia make in lines 16 -17 (*"The doctor . . . numbers."*)?

   A. Change *The doctor* to **The doctors**.
   B. Change *people* to **poeple**.
   C. Change *hedaches* to **headaches**.
   D. The sentence is all right as it is.

8. Tia wants to add another sentence at the end of the last paragraph. Which of the following sentences would make the best last line?

   A. I don't see why we can't do it.
   B. Head injuries are serious, no matter what age you are.
   C. Children get better quicker.
   D. Children and people of all ages need to bike safely.

Antonio wrote the following book report for his English class. Read the report carefully and help him improve his organization, revise his sentence structure, and correct his mechanics. Feel free to write in the text as you read, revise, and edit the report.

1   <u>WARRIORS</u>

2   A Book Report by Antonio Torivio

3   The book <u>Warriors</u> by Kenji kawano tells about how the United

4   States Army used Native American soldiers from the Navajo tribe

5   to confuse the Japanese in World War II. This book is all about

6   how codes are made.   By using their Navajo language, the code

7   could not be understood by the Germans or the Japanese.

8   There job was dangerous and difficult. They often landed with

9   the first group of soldiers, and immediately setting up their

10   radios. Soon they were sending back information about the

11   landing and about the size of the enemy forces. Battle planners

12   used this information. To make decisions about where to send

13   more soldiers. Lugging eighty pounds of equipment, they were

14   often shot at. The book describes how courageous they were.

15   The idea of using the Navajo soldiers in this way was

16   suggested by Philip Johnston. Johnston was not an Indian. He

17   had grown up on the Navajo Reservation. And could speak

18   Navajo. When he learned that the Army needed a new code, he

19   remembered the time he been a translator for some Navajos.

20   The Navajo code was never broken. For more than twenty

21   years the government and code talkers kept their secret. They

22   were allowed to talk about it. Now, every year, they are honored

23   by marching in a big parade in Gallup, New Mexico.

9. Which revision, if any, should Antonio make in line 3 ("*The book . . . United*")?

   A. Change **_Warriors_** to "**Warriors**."
   B. Change **_Kenji kawano_** to **kenji kawano**.
   C. Change **_United_** to **united**.
   D. Change **_Kenji kawano_** to **Kenji Kawano**.

10. Which revision should Antonio make in the sentence in lines 6-7 ("*By using . . . Japanese.*")?

    A. By using their Navajo language, the soldiers could
    B. By using their own language, the code could
    C. When they used their own language, they could
    D. Using their own language, the code

11. What revision, if any, should Antonio make in the sentence in line 8 ("*There . . . difficult.*")

    A. Change **_There_** to **They're**.
    B. Change **_There_** to **Their**.
    C. Change **_There_** to **They**.
    D. Make no change.

12. The sentence in lines 12-13 ("*To . . . soldiers.*") is a fragment. Which of the following sentences would be the best revision?

    A. Battle planners used this information; to make decisions about where to send more soldiers.
    B. Battle planners used this information, to make decisions about where to send more soldiers.
    C. Battle planners used this information, and they made decisions about where to send more soldiers.
    D. Battle planners used this information to make decisions about where to send more soldiers.

13. Which is the best way to combine the three sentences in lines 16-18 ("*Johnston . . . Navajo.*")?

    A. Although Johnston was not an Indian, he had grown up on the Navajo Reservation and could speak Navajo.
    B. Because Johnston had grown up on the Navajo Reservation, he could speak Navajo.
    C. Johnston was not an Indian he had grown up on the Navajo Reservation and could speak Navajo.
    D. While Johnston was not an Indian, he had grown up on the Navajo Reservation.

14. Which transitional word or phrase does Antonio need at the beginning of the sentence in lines 21-22 ("*They . . . it.*")?

    A. First,
    B. Finally,
    C. As a result,
    D. Nevertheless,

15. The sentence that could be omitted from Antonio's book report because it does NOT support the focus of the report is the one in lines

    A. 5-6 ("*This book . . . made.*")
    B. 14 ("*The book describes . . . were.*")
    C. 20 ("*The Navajo code . . . broken.*")
    D. 22-23 ("*Now, every year . . . Mexico.*")

16. Antonio wants to add the following paragraph to his essay. What would be the best location for this paragraph?

    I liked this book a lot because I learned how important the Navajo language was in World War II. Anyone interested in Native Americans or in war stories would enjoy this book.

    A. between paragraphs 1 and 2.
    B. between paragraphs 2 and 3.
    C. between paragraphs 3 and 4.
    D. after paragraph 4.

PASSAGE I

Natali has written this letter to Ms. Emily, who writes an advice column for a local paper. Natali has asked you to review it before she sends it.

Read the letter carefully and help Natali improve her organization, revise her sentence structure, and correct her mechanics. Feel free to write in the text as you read, revise, and edit the letter.

1   March 15, 199-

2   Dear Ms. Emily:

3   I have a problem. The problem is with my friends. They

4   don't want to be my friends any more. Jackie says that I'm

5   conceited and stuckup because I don't have time for lunch.

6   Carla is on the basketball team. Dariel wants me to share a

7   babysitting job with her. Although she knows I have dance

8   practice every day. My mother suggested that I write to you.

9   About my friends what do you think I should do? How can

10   I make them understand? I have wanted to be a professional

11   dancer since I was nine. I saw the New Jersey Ballet Company

12   one Christmas vacation and begun to take lessons. This

13   summer I started taking dance very serious. My teacher says if

14   I continue to work hard I have a chance of making it. I will

15   have to spend all my free time practicing.

16   My older brother Tom says that I need some new friends.

17   That may be true but where will I get them? Jackie and

18   Dariel have been my friends since third grade. I wish they

19   would understand. Ms. Emily do you think I should take my

20   brother's advice? Or can you help me keep my old friends?

21   Sincerely,

22   Lonely Dancer

17. Which sentence below best combines the three sentences in lines 3-4 ("*I . . . any more.*")?

   A. I have a problem with my friends they aren't my friends anymore.
   B. I have a problem with my friends; they don't want to be friends any more.
   C. I have a problem with friends who don't want to be my friends any more.
   D. My friends are not my friends any more.

18. You notice that Natali has written a sentence fragment in the sentence in lines 7-8 ("*Although . . . day.*") Which of the following sentences would be the best revision?

   A. Dariel wants me to share a babysitting job with her she knows I have dance practice every day.
   B. Dariel wants me to share a babysitting job with her although she knows I have dance practice every day.
   C. Dariel wants me to share a babysitting job with her; she knows I have dance practice every day.
   D. Dariel wants me to share a babysitting job with her and she knows I have dance practice every day.

19. How should Natali revise the sentence in line 9 ("*About . . . do?*")?

   A. About my friends what do you think I should have done?
   B. What do you think I should do about my friends?
   C. What do you think I should have done about my friends?
   D. Make no change.

20. Which revision, if any, should Natali make to the sentence in lines 11-12 ("*I . . . lessons.*")?

   A. Change *and begun* to **and have begun**.
   B. Change *and begun* to **and am beginning**.
   C. Change *and begun* to **and began**.
   D. Make no change.

21. What is the best revision for line 12-13 ("*This . . . serious.*")?

   A. This summer, I started taking dance very serious.
   B. This summer I have started taking dance more serious.
   C. This summer I have started taking dance very seriously.
   D. This summer I started to take dance serious.

22. What editing change, if any, is needed in line 17 ("*That . . . them*")?

   A. Add a **comma** after *true*.
   B. Add a **semicolon** after *true*.
   C. Change the **question mark** to a **period**.
   D. Make no change.

23. What editing change, if any, is needed in lines 19-20 ("*Ms. Emily . . . advice?*")?

   A. Change the **question mark** to a **period**.
   B. Add a **comma** after *Ms. Emily*.
   C. Omit the **apostrophe** from *brother's*.
   D. Make no change.

24. Which sentence, if any, should be omitted from Natali's letter?

   A. Omit the last sentence in paragraph 3.
   B. Omit the sentence in line 6 ("*Carla . . . team.*")
   C. Omit the sentence in lines 9-10 ("*How . . . understand?*")
   D. Make no change.

PASSAGE J

Shakila wrote the following review of a TV movie for her history class. She asked you to look it over for her and help her improve it before she hands it in.

Read the review carefully and help her improve her organization, revise her sentence structure, and correct her mechanics. Feel free to write in the text as you read and edit the review.

1   Channel 12 has a new series called <u>Black Cowboys of the</u>

2   <u>Old West</u>. It's about black cowboys. It tells a lot about what

3   America was like. If you don't know very much about the

4   Old West, you will like this series.

5   The first story was about a Wyoming cowboy named Bronco

6   Sam. He said, I can ride anything on four legs. He proved it

7   time after time. His friends made bets on his ability to

8   ride. One day, Bronco Sam's friends dared him to ride through

9   town on a wild bull.   Sam was on the back of a bucking steer,

10   headed through Cheyenne.

11   The steer saw its reflection in the glass window of a

12   clothing store. It charged through the window and ran up

13   and down the aisles. Then it shot back out through the broken

14   window, dragging clothing on its horns. Sam rode the bull

15   back to the ranch. The next day, the storekeeper sent him a bill

16   for three hundred dollars. Which Sam paid right away.

17   I liked this show. It was funny. Sometimes history shows are

18   too serious, although this one wasn't. It also made the Old

19   West very real to me. Next week's show is about an African-

20   American cowboy who could rope anything he saw. The part

21   will be played by my favorite actor Eddie Jackson. If you're

22   interested in American history, you'll want to watch.

25. What editing change, if any, should Shakila make in lines 1-2 of her review?

   A. Change <u>Black Cowboys of the Old West</u> to <u>Black cowboys of the Old West</u>.
   B. Change <u>Black Cowboys of the Old West</u> to <u>Black Cowboys of the old West</u>.
   C. Change <u>Black Cowboys of the Old West</u> to <u>Black Cowboys of the old west</u>.
   D. Make no change

26. How should Shakila revise the sentence in lines 2-3 ("*It . . . like.*") to make it clearer?

   A. It tells a lot about what America was like over a hundred years ago in the past.
   B. It tells a lot about what America was really like.
   C. It tells a lot about what Americans were like.
   D. It tells a lot about what America was like over a hundred years ago.

27. What editing change does Shakila need to make in the sentence in line 6 ("*He . . . legs.*")?

   A. Take out the **comma** following the word ***said***.
   B. Add **quotation marks** before the word ***I***.
   C. Add **quotation marks** before the word ***I*** and after ***legs***.
   D. Change the **period** to a **question mark**.

28. What transition word is needed at the beginning of the sentence on lines 9-10 ("*Sam . . . Cheyenne.*").

   A. After,
   B. Soon,
   C. However,
   D. Because,

29. What is the best way to combine the first two sentences in the third paragraph?

   A. The steer saw its reflection in the glass window of the clothing store, and it charged through the window and ran up and down the aisles.
   B. Although the steer saw its reflection in the glass window of the clothing store, it charged through the window and ran up and down the aisles.
   C. When the steer saw its reflection in the glass window of the clothing store, it charged through the window and ran up and down the aisles.
   D. The steer saw its reflection in the glass window of the clothing store, but it charged through the window and ran up and down the aisles.

30. How would you revise the two sentences in lines 15-16 ("*The next day . . . away.*")?

   A. The next day Sam paid the store keeper three hundred dollars.
   B. The next day, the storekeeper sent him a bill for three hundred dollars, which Sam paid right away.
   C. Sam paid the bill right away after the storekeeper sent it to him.
   D. Make no change.

31. How should Shakila combine the first two sentences in paragraph 4 ("*I . . . funny.*")?

   A. I liked this show, and it was funny.
   B. Because it was funny I liked the show.
   C. I liked this show because it was funny.
   D. Although it was funny, I liked the show.

32. What editing change, if any, should Shakila make in the sentence on lines 20-21 ("*The . . . Jackson.*")?

   A. Add a **comma** after ***actor***.
   B. Change ***will be*** to **was**.
   C. Change ***favorite*** to **favorit**.
   D. Make no change.

PASSAGE K

Vince has written this letter to a toy company to complain about one of their products. He has asked you to look over the letter and help him improve it before he sends it.

Read the letter carefully and help Vince improve his organization, revise his sentence structure, and correct his mechanics. Feel free to write in the text as you read, revise, and edit the letter.

1   April 16, 199–

2   Dear Science Toys:

3   I am very disappointed in your product. Wanting to be a

4   crime fighter when he grows up, I thought it would be a

5   perfect present for my brother. It said right on the box that

6   Detecto Lab was easy to put together. It also said that the lie

7   detector really works. Wrong.

8   Please send me the kit right away. My brother jumped for

9   joy when he opened the present. Oh, boy, I can be a detective

10   right now, he said. It took us three hours to put the kit

11   together. Nine year olds don't like to wait that long. We put in

12   the right batteries too. Nothing worked. The lie detector

13   didn't light up the fingerprint powder was all caked up. The

14   instruction book looked like it wasn't even written in English.

15   I would like a new kit that works. Second, I think I should

16   not have to pay postage for it. Do you enjoy disappointing

17   kids?

18   Sincerely yours,

19   Vince Robertson

33. How should Vince revise the first sentence of paragraph 1 (line 3) to make it more logical?

   A. I am very disappointed in your product because it isn't good.

   B. I am very disappointed in your product Detecto Lab.

   C. I am very disappointed in your excellent product Detecto Lab.

   D. I am very disappointed that you made this product.

34. What is the best revision, if any, of lines 3-4 ("Wanting . . . present.")?

   A. I wanted to be a crime fighter when I grow up so I thought it would be a perfect present for my brother.

   B. I thought it would be a perfect present for him wanting to be a crime fighter when he grows up.

   C. Because he wants to be a crime fighter when he grows up, I thought it would be a perfect present for my brother.

   D. Make no change.

35. What is the best way for Vince to correct the fragment in line 7 ("Wrong.")?

   A. Both statements are wrong.
   B. Wrong on both counts.
   C. It was wrong.
   D. Nothing is wrong.

36. What would be the best location of the first sentence in paragraph 2 (line 8)?

   A. It should be the first sentence in the first paragraph (line 3).

   B. It should be the last sentence in the third paragraph (line 17).

   C. It should be the last sentence in the second paragraph (line 14-15)

   D. The sentence is best left where it is.

37. What editing change is needed in lines 9-10 ("Oh . . . said.")?

   A. Add **quotation marks** before **Oh**.
   B. Add a **question mark** after **said**.
   C. Add **quotation marks** before **Oh** and after **now,**
   D. Omit the **commas** before and after **boy**.

38. You notice a run-on sentence in lines 12-13 ("The . . . up.") Which revision will you suggest to Vince?

   A. The lie detector didn't light up, so the fingerprint powder was all caked up.

   B. The lie detector didn't light up, and the fingerprint powder was all caked up.

   C. The lie detector didn't light up, the fingerprint powder was all caked up.

   D. The lie detector didn't light up, but the fingerprint powder was all caked up.

39. Which transition word should Vince use to introduce the last paragraph (line 15)?

   A. Now,
   B. First,
   C. Finally,
   D. Also,

40. Which sentence does not belong in this letter?

   A. (lines 6-7) *It also said that the lie detector really works.*

   B. (lines 10-11) *It took us three hours to put the kit together.*

   C. (line 12) *Nothing worked.*

   D. (lines 16-17) *Do you enjoy disappointing kids?*

PASSAGE L

Meagan has written a letter to her cousin Maggie, whom she met for the first time last summer. Meagan wants Maggie to come for a visit and hopes the letter will persuade Maggie and her parents to let her come. She has asked you to look over the first draft.

Read her letter carefully and help her improve her organization, revise her sentence structure, and correct her mechanics. Feel free to write in the text as you read, revise, and edit the letter.

1   March 2, 199–

2   Dear Maggie,

3   I'm glad we finaly met after all these years. Living in

4   California we didn't get a chance to meet you until we took our

5   trip to Disneyland. Now its your turn to visit. Can you come in

6   June? If you can't, how about April vacation?

7   We can go shopping at the mall. We can go to the

8   amusement park I told you about. We can go to New York City.

9   You've never tasted real New Jersey pizza. When you have your

10   first slice, you'll never want California pizza again. I like

11   your tacos though. Also the weather.

12   There's so much to do that it will take more than a week.

13   Can you stay? Your parents could come out in August

14   and spend time with my Dad and I. I know he'd like that too.

15   Your Mom was always his favorite sister.

16   Thanks for the letters and my birthday present. I really liked

17   it alot. Let me hear from you soon.

18   Your newfound cousin,

19   Meagan

41. What editing change, if any, should Meagan make in line 3 ("*I'm . . . years.*")?

    A. Put a **comma** before *after*.
    B. Change *finaly* to **finally**.
    C. Add **even** before *after*.
    D. Make no change.

42. What change should Meagan make in lines 3-4 ("*Living . . . Disneyland.*") to clarify the meaning?

    A. Since you live in California, we didn't get a chance to meet you until we took our trip to Disneyland.
    B. Since living in California, we didn't get a chance to meet you until we took our trip to Disneyland.
    C. We didn't get a chance to meet you until we took our trip to Disneyland.
    D. We never met you until we took our trip to Disneyland.

43. What editing change, if any, should Meagan make in line 5 ("*Now . . . visit.*")?

    A. Change *its* to **it's**.
    B. Add a **comma** after *Now*.
    C. Change the **period** to a **question mark**.
    D. Make no change.

44. What is the best way to combine the sentences in lines 7-8 ("*We . . . City.*")?

    A. We can go shopping, to the amusement park, and New York City.
    B. We can shop at the mall, spend a day at an amusement park, and visit New York City.
    C. We can shop and visit an amusement park and New York City.
    D. We can see the mall, an amusement park, and to visit New York City.

45. What transitional word should Meagan begin line 9 with ("*You've . . . pizza.*")?

    A. Since,
    B. Also,
    C. And,
    D. But

46. What is the best way to fix the fragment in line 11 ("*Also the weather.*")?

    A. I like your tacos also weather.
    B. I like your tacos though. I also like your weather.
    C. I like your tacos. Though the weather.
    D. I like your tacos; also weather.

47. Which revision makes the sentence in line 13 ("*Can you stay?*") more logical?

    A. Can you stay in June?
    B. Can you stay for the whole summer?
    C. Can you stay with us?
    D. Can you stay in New Jersey?

48. What editing change, if any, should Meagan make in lines 16-17 ("*I . . . alot.*")?

    A. Change *liked* to **have liked**.
    B. Change *alot* to **a lot**.
    C. Change *really* to **realy**.
    D. Make no change.

Skills and Practice Handbook

CAPITALIZATION

Memorize and use these five capitalization rules. You should be able to identify and correct any errors that involve these rules.

1. **Courtesy titles.** Capitalize courtesy titles when used before a person's name.

> Ms. Jackson
>
> Governor Jackson
>
> Dr. Augusta Rucker
>
> Senator Braun
>
> Mr. Abrams

✎ Write three names with titles:

_____

_____

_____

2. **Words in the title of a written work.** Capitalize the first word in the title and all other words *except* very short words like the following:

> a, an, the (*articles*)
>
> of, at, in, on, to, with (*short prepositions*)
>
> and, or, but, nor, for, yet, so (*short coordinating conjunctions*)
>
> The Adventures of Tom Sawyer
>
> To Kill a Mockingbird

✎ Write the title of a book or a movie:

_____

3. **Proper nouns.** A proper noun is the name of a specific person, place, or thing. Capitalize all parts of the name, except for words like *the, of, and*. Place names are particularly important.

✎ Beside each example below, write one of your own:

Persons

    Thomas Edison   _____

Places

    United States of America   _____

    Asia   _____

    Lake Hopatcong   _____

    Delaware River   _____

    East Rutherford   _____

    Montclair High School   _____

    Broad Street   _____

    Atlantic Ocean   _____

    Kittatinny Mountains   _____

    Garden State Parkway   _____

Languages

    Spanish   _____

Nationalities/Ethnic groups

    African-American   _____

Calendar names and holidays

    Tuesday   _____

    March   _____

    Independence Day   _____

Historical events

    the American Revolution   _____

Political groups, companies, and organizations

    Republicans   _____

Summit Savings Bank _____

Boy Scouts of America _____

4. **Proper Adjectives.** Capitalize proper adjectives, which are formed from proper nouns—usually from place names. Notice that the words they refer to are <u>not</u> capitalized.

    Arabic language _____

5. **First word in a direct quotation.** Capitalize the first word in a direct quotation, even when it is in the middle of a sentence.

    "Have you come to see the play?" asked the usher.

    Ernesto said, "I'm waiting for my sister."

_____

_____

✎ CAPITALIZATION PRACTICE TEST

Circle the number of each sentence that contains a capitalization error.

1. Here comes mr. Higgins.
2. We went to see *Gone With The Wind*.
3. The speaker will be governor Ellen Whitaker.
4. Connie lives in west paterson.
5. Have you ever been to the Franklin Museum?
6. The Republicans and the democrats agreed to work together.
7. David wanted to learn how to cook chinese food.
8. "please turn off the engine when the light goes on," said the driving teacher.
9. Deena asked, "Has anyone seen my math book?"
10. We're having a party at 376 park Street.

PUNCTUATION

Memorize and use these punctuation rules. You should be able to identify and correct any errors that involve these rules.

✎ Look at each example. Write a similar example of your own in the spaces provided. Have a partner check your work.

A. END PUNCTUATION

    1. Period. Put a period at the end of a sentence that is a statement or a command.

        The sun is a star. _____

        Please open the door. _____

        Come in. _____

    2. Question mark. Use a question mark at the end of a direct question.

        What time is it? _____

B. COMMA. You should know these nine comma rules.

    1. Between independent clauses joined by a coordinating conjunction.

The comma goes before the conjunction.

You should memorize the coordinating conjunctions:

    and, but, or, nor, for, yet, so.

Each independent clause could stand alone as a complete sentence.

    I pushed the button, but nothing happened.

    We can go to the movies, or we can just stay home.

✎ Write two sentences of your own. Have a partner check your work.

_____

_____

2. **To separate coordinate adjectives.** Put a comma between adjectives— if you could use the word *and* between them instead of a comma.

   her open, smiling face ("Her open and smiling face" sounds natural.)

   a rough, windy day

✎ Write two phrases like the ones above in which you put a comma between the adjectives.

_____

_____

If the word *and* would not sound natural between the adjectives, don't put in a comma.

   a cute little baby ("A cute and little baby" doesn't sound natural.)

   the good old days

✎ Write two phrases like the ones above in which you do not put a comma between the adjectives.

_____

_____

3. **To set off an appositive.** (An appositive is a noun phrase that stands next to another noun and gives additional information about it.)

   Ms. Santaria, our history teacher, is planning a conference.

✎ Write a sentence of your own that contains an appositive. Ask a partner to check your work.

_____

4. **Between the name of a city and a state.**

   Trenton, New Jersey   _____

   Butte, Montana   _____

5. **Before a direct quotation.** The comma goes after the words that identify the speaker.

   Bill asked, "When do we start?"

   I answered quickly, "In a minute."

✎ Write two sentences of your own that contain direct quotations. Ask a partner to check your work.

_____

_____

6. **To set off a name in direct address.** Use a comma to set off a person's name when he or she is being spoken to. (A name used this way is called a noun of address.)

> Yes, Mr. Greene, I can hear you.

> Do you think so, Martha?

✎ Write two sentences of your own. Check your work with a partner.

_____

_____

7. **After an introductory word or group of words.** Use a comma after an introductory word that doesn't have a strong connection to the rest of the sentence.

> Well, I guess so.

> Yes, I know.

✎ Write two sentences of your own. Check your work with a partner.

_____

_____

8. **After an introductory participial phrase.** A *participial phrase* is a phrase built around a verb form known as a *participle*. There are two kinds of participles, present and past.

> **Present**   ends in *-ing:*
>
> eating   taking   loving   fooling
>
> **Past**   the form that follows *have* or *has*:
>
> eaten   taken   loved   fooled

129

Walking alone, I finally had time to look at the scenery.

Hated by everyone, the dictator fled the country.

✎ Write two sentences of your own that contain introductory participial phrases. Check your work with a partner.

_____

_____

9. **After an introductory dependent clause.** A dependent clause is usually introduced by words like *if, because, although, after, before, when.*

If we leave early, we'll get there before noon.

Before you know it, the job will be done.

✎ Write two sentences of your own that contain dependent clauses. Check your work with a partner.

_____

_____

✎ COMMA PRACTICE TEST

Rewrite each sentence, inserting commas where necessary. Be ready to explain which comma rule you are using.

1. Rajiv made two touchdowns but we lost anyway.

2. Arlene can you edit my work for me?

3. Leroy a skillful carpenter built those shelves.

4. The baby gave us a happy toothless grin.

5. When did they move to Shelby Montana?

6. Jumping the curb the car slammed into the fence.

7. Bill suggested "Maybe we took the wrong turn."

8. Bored with the party Gil fell asleep on the sofa.

9. How far is it to Yuba City California?

10. Tossed by the storm the little boat was close to sinking.

11. Yes the books you ordered have finally arrived.

12. Stars gleamed overhead and fireflies twinkled on the lawn.

13. Ricardo please turn down that radio.

14. Terrie asked worriedly "Where are we now?"

15. Well I just hope you're right.

16. Having finished her work early Nancy went for a bike ride.

17. Kate can you answer the question?

18. Soo-lin plays the piano and her sister plays the guitar.

19. By the way Alice is a very good basketball player.

20. When Lisa gets to Denver she will call us.

C. SEMICOLON

Use a semicolon to separate independent clauses not joined by a coordinating conjunction.

I ran; Jack followed.

The car won't start; I guess we'll have to walk.

[NOTE: A semicolon is often used to correct a run-on sentence. See pages 136-37.]

✎Write two sentences of your own that contain semicolons. Check your work with a partner.

_____

_____

D. APOSTROPHE

Use an apostrophe in the following places.

✎After each example, write a similar one of your own.

1. In possessives

a day's work   _____

the students' ideas _____

children's toys   _____

someone's mistake   _____

WARNING: The possessives of personal pronouns **do not** contain apostrophes. The possessive **its** never has an apostrophe.

his dog   _____

her cat   _____

its collar   _____

2. **In contractions.** Put an apostrophe in a contraction in place of the letter or letters that are dropped.

     isn't   _____

     it's   _____

     I'm   _____

     you're   _____

WARNING:

     Its is the possessive of **it**.

     It's is the contraction of **it is**.

E. COLON

Use a colon—

Before a list of words or phrases.

Be sure to bring the necessary tools: a hammer, a saw, and a tape measure.

These are my plans: to go to law school, to become governor of New Jersey, and to win a Grammy award for best new musician.

✎ Write two sentences of your own that use a colon. Check your work with a partner.

_____

_____

_____

_____

F. QUOTATION MARKS

Use quotation marks in the following places.

1. At the beginning and end of a direct quotation from a text or speech.

Shakespeare's play *Hamlet* contains one of his most famous quotes: "To be or not to be, that is the question."

"Your eyes are like two deep blue lakes," Eric said to his girlfriend.

✎ Write two sentences of your own. Check your work with a partner.

_____

_____

_____

_____

2. Enclosing the titles of articles, essays, short stories, and poems.

Have you read Willa Cather's story "Paul's Case"?

I liked the article "The New Jersey Hills."

✎ Write two sentences of your own that contain titles of short works. Check your sentences with a partner.

_____

_____

✎ PUNCTUATION PRACTICE TEST

Rewrite each sentence, adding semicolons, colons, apostrophes, and quotation marks where they are needed. Be ready to explain which rule you are using.

1. Currently, China is the world's most populous country by 2100 India is expected to surpass it.

2. Meagan hasnt been feeling well lately.

3. Here are the ingredients red pepper flakes, tomato paste, and cheese.

4. What you need most is a good nights sleep.

5. The poet Emma Lazarus wrote the line Send me your tired, your poor, the wretched refuse of your teeming shores.

6. Its a long time since we heard from Julio.

7. Chinese, English, French, Russian, and Spanish were the first official languages of the United Nations Arabic was added in 1973.

8. Its time to go to work.

9. Be sure you have the following items with you extra socks, a rain poncho, a water bottle, and a light sweater.

10. The cars front end was out of alignment.

11. My favorite poem by Robert Frost is Stopping by Woods on a Snowy Evening.

12. All I know Simon said is that I didn't do it.

13. Kareem complained Somebody ate all the ice cream.

14. The girls hockey team is still undefeated.

15. Will is upstairs Sam is in the kitchen.

SENTENCE CONSTRUCTION

You should be able to select a revision that corrects the following errors in sentence construction.

A. INCORRECT AND INCONSISTENT VERB USAGE AND PRONOUN USAGE

1. Agreement

Rule 1: A subject must agree with its verb.

Incorrect: One of those men are on the team.

To correct: Find the subject of the sentence. Don't be distracted by the phrase (*of those men*) that comes between the subject (*one*) and the verb. The subject is singular; therefore, the verb should be singular (*is*).

✎ **Make the revision:**

_____

Rule 2: A pronoun must agree with its antecedent.

Incorrect: Each of the girls should bring their own lunch.

To correct: Find the subject of the sentence. Don't be distracted by the phrase (*of the girls*) that comes between the subject (*each*) and the possessive pronoun. The subject is singular; therefore the pronoun should be singular (*her*).

✎ **Make the revision:**

_____

2. Tense formation

Rule 1: Use the appropriate tense.

Incorrect: Sid walks two miles before I got up this morning.

To correct: When did Sid walk? Before I got up this morning. Therefore, the verb should be in the past tense (*walked*)

✎ **Make the revision:**

_____

Rule 2: Use the proper form of irregular verbs.

Incorrect: The senator has often spoke on that subject.

To correct: The verb *speak* is an irregular verb. The form to use is *has spoken*.

✎ **Make the revision:**

_____

3. Pronouns

Rule 1: A subject pronoun must be used for the subject of a sentence or a clause.

Incorrect: You and him are next in line.

To correct: The correct form is *You and he.*

✎ **Make the revision:**

_____

135

Rule 2: An object pronoun must be used for the direct or indirect object of a verb or the object of a preposition.

Incorrect: Let's keep this between you and I.

To correct: The correct form is *between you and me*.

✎ **Make the revision:**

_____

Rule 3: A possessive pronoun must be used to show possession and must be formed correctly.

Incorrect: The cat arched it's back.

To correct: The correct form is *its*.

✎ **Make the revision:**

_____

B. SENTENCE FRAGMENTS AND RUN-ON SENTENCES

1. Sentence fragments

Rule: A complete sentence always has a subject and a predicate.

Incorrect: Bill came into the room. Without his shoes on.

To correct: The second "sentence" is a sentence fragment. This one lacks <u>both</u> a subject and a predicate. It is really part of the sentence before it.

✎ **Make the revision:**

_____

2. Run-on sentences

Rule: Avoid stringing sentences together without proper punctuation or without using conjunctions.

Incorrect: The team has won all its home games it is not so lucky away.

To correct: You can fix a run-on by using a semicolon to separate the two sentences. Or you can use a conjunction like *but* with a comma preceding it.

**Make the revision** (Try both ways):

_____

_____

C. INCORRECT USE OF MODIFIERS AND MODIFYING PHRASES

1. Comparative and superlative forms

Rule 1: Use the *-er* form when comparing two items; use the *-est* form when comparing more than two.

Incorrect: Jessie is the oldest of two sisters.

To correct: Only two items are being compared. Use the *-er* form.

**Make the revision:**

_____

Rule 2: When the adjective has two or more syllables, use *more* or *most* to form comparisons.

Incorrect: I feel even terribler today than I did yesterday.

To correct: The word *terrible* is more than two syllables. Use *more* instead of *-er*.

Make the revision:

_____

(EXCEPTION: When a two-syllable adjective ends in the letter *-y*, it often takes the endings *-er* and *-est: funny, funnier, funniest*)

2. Modifier usage

Rule: Adjectives modify nouns or pronouns. Adverbs modify verb, adjectives, or other adverbs.

Incorrect: Rene walked very quiet.

To correct: Use the adverb form of quiet to modify the verb walked.

✎ **Make the revision**:

_____

3. Misplacement of modifiers

Rule: Modifiers must be near the words they modify.

Incorrect: We gave a new set of tools to the stage crew, which was very expensive.

To correct: The meaning is unclear. Are the tools expensive or is the stage crew expensive? You can make the meaning clearer by moving the modifying phrase (*which was very expensive*).

✎ **Make the revision**:

_____

D. INCORRECT USE OF PARALLEL STRUCTURE

Rule: Use phrases that have the same structure to make your sentences balanced.

Incorrect: To make strawberry shortcake, you need strawberries, whipped cream, and to bake some biscuits.

To correct: The phrase *to bake some biscuits* is different from the other objects in the sentence (*strawberries, whipped cream*). You can make the sentence parallel by changing the phrase to a noun.

✎ **Make the revision**:

_____

E. INCORRECT COORDINATION AND SUBORDINATION OF IDEAS

Rule: When you revise, make sure that the ideas are placed in an order that shows which thoughts are more important than others.

Incorrect: There was a test the next day, and Myra prepared for it, frowning in concentration.

To correct: The idea that Myra was preparing for a text the next day should be subordinated to the idea that Myra frowned in concentration. The present participle *preparing* can begin the revised sentence.

✎ **Make the revision:**

_____

F. INCORRECT USE OF STANDARD WRITTEN ENGLISH

Rule: Use standard English when you write.

Incorrect: There isn't nothing we can do about it now.

To correct: This sentence contains a double negative (*isn't, nothing*), which is incorrect in standard English. Make it correct by removing one of the negatives.

✎ **Make the revision:**

_____

G. WORDY OR IMPRECISE LANGUAGE

Rule 1: Use concise language. Do not be wordy.

Incorrect: Alex was late because of the fact that he missed the bus.

To correct: The phrase *of the fact that* adds nothing to the sentence. You can remove it and the sentence will mean the same.

✎ **Make the revision:**

_____

Rule 2: Use precise language. Do not use words and phrases that are too vague or general.

   Incorrect: It was a nice day.

   To correct: The word *nice* is too vague. The writer must add details that supply specific meaning.

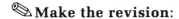 **Make the revision:**

_____

SENTENCE COMBINING

Some changes you make in text are not based on rules of writing but on logic. Always ask yourself, Do I understand what the writer means? What can I add or change to make the meaning clearer?

On the EWT you may be asked to select a revision that makes one of the following changes in sentences.

1. Completing a partially constructed sentence by adding words, phrases, or clauses that extend the logic of the text.

   Sentence that needs more information: <u>With George Washington at Valley Forge</u> is a book about the Army. It takes place in 1777 and 1778.

   To improve: The first sentence in the example is too general. A reader would want to know, which Army? During what war?

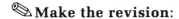 **Make the revision:**

_____

_____

2. Combining written text to make it more concise or cohesive.

   Uncombined: The house was deserted. It was old. It looked scary.

   To combine: When you combine ideas into one sentence, be sure you keep the meaning. You will need to choose a revision that contains the key words *deserted*, *old*, and *scary*.

 **Make the revision:**

   _____

3. Making clearer, logical transitions by using specific transition words, phrases, or sentences.

   The following are common words and phrases that help show logical connections between sentences or between ideas.

   - **Compare and contrast**— *though, although, on the one hand, in the same way, instead, however, on the other hand,*
   - **Show cause and effect**— *as a result, therefore, consequently, because, since, for this reason*
   - **Show time**— *that day, later, earlier, now, then, at the same time, meanwhile*
   - **Show how often**—*usually, never, occasionally, sometimes, often*
   - **Summarize/conclude**— *therefore, consequently, finally, in conclusion, after all*
   - **Show alternatives**— *of course, certainly, however, nevertheless*
   - **Illustrate a point**— *also, along with, for instance, for example, in addition, in other words, also, besides, as well. in fact, in the first place*
   - **Show a sequence or a process**— *then, next, following, later, finally, first, second, third*

   Weak logical connection: Ida broke the window. She needed a new pane of glass.

   To show a stronger logical connection: These two sentences are logically connected. What transitional word or phrase will express the connection best? Since the first sentence causes the action in the second sentence, choose a word that shows cause.

    **Make the revision:**

   _____

ORGANIZING IDEAS

The final multiple-choice question on an EWT writing passage is often a question about the passage as a whole. Here are some examples:

- Which of the following sentences <u>best</u> states the controlling idea of this passage?

- Which of the following would be the <u>best</u> last sentence for the passage?

- Which sentence would be the <u>best</u> to omit from the passage?

To answer questions like these, you must have a good sense of the meaning and purpose of the passage as a whole. Read the passage carefully and be sure you understand it before you answer this kind of question.